BEADS *and* STRANDS

Books Published
by Orbis Books
in the
Theology in Africa Series

In keeping with its mission to publish works by authors from the Third World (or "Global South") Orbis Books collaborates with Regnum Africa in Ghana and Editions Clé in Cameroun to bring outstanding works on African theology and religious reflection from both Francophone and Anglophone Africa. These books are part of these two publishers' "Theological Reflections from the South" Series, which may in time include books from Asia and Latin America.

Other books published in the Series

Kwame Bediako, *Jesus and the Gospel in Africa*: *History and Experience*

Kä Mana, *Christians and Churches of Africa: Salvation in Christ and Building a New African Society.*

Theology in Africa Series

BEADS *and* STRANDS
REFLECTIONS OF AN AFRICAN WOMAN
ON CHRISTIANITY IN AFRICA

Mercy Amba Oduyoye

ORBIS BOOKS
Maryknoll, New York 10545

regnum
africa

Founded in 1970, Orbis Books endeavors to publish works that enlighten the mind, nourish the spirit, and challenge the conscience. The publishing arm of the Maryknoll Fathers and Brothers, Orbis seeks to explore the global dimensions of the Christian faith and mission, to invite dialogue with diverse cultures and religious traditions, and to serve the cause of reconciliation and peace. The books published reflect the opinions of their authors and are not meant to represent the official position of the Maryknoll Society. To obtain more information about Maryknoll and Orbis Books, please visit our website at www.maryknoll.org.

Published by Orbis Books, Maryknoll, New York, U.S.A. All rights reserved.

First published in 2002 in the "Theological Reflections from the South" Series by Editions Clé (B.P. 1501, Yaoundé, Cameroun) and Regnum Africa (P. O. Box 76, Akrpong-Akuapem, Ghana), as part of Regnum Books International (P.O. Box 70 Oxford OX2 6HB, United Kingdom) for the International Fellowship of Evangelical Mission Theologians, formed of the African Theological Fellowship, the Latin American Theological Fraternity (José Marmol 1734, 1602 Florida, Buenos Aires, Argentina), and Partnership in Mission Asia (P. B. 21, Vasant Vihar, New Delhi 110 057, India)

Manufactured in the United States of America.

Library of Congress Cataloging in Publication Data

Oduyoye, Mercy Amba.
    Beads and strands : reflections of an African woman on Christianity in Africa / Mercy Amba Oduyoye.
        p. cm.
    Includes bibliographical references.
    ISBN 1-57075-543-4 (pbk.)
        1. Christianity—Africa. 2. Women in Christianity—Africa. I. Title.

BR1360.O36 2004
276'.082—dc22

2004049551

Contents

PART III
WOMEN, TRADITION AND THE GOSPEL IN AFRICA

Acknowledgements

Materials in this book have been presented and published in earlier forms. I am grateful to the editors publishers for permission to edit and focus them for this volume. I hope that the collecting, editing and abridgement in this volume will make them accessible between two covers for a variety of church and school uses. Chapter 1, abridged here, was first published in my *Hearing and Knowing: Theological Reflections on Christianity in Africa* (Maryknoll, N.Y.: Orbis Books, 1986): 70-89 Chapter 2 is abridged from *Hearing and Knowing* (ibid.): 90-96, ; Chapter 3 is abridged from *Hearing and Knowing* (ibid.): 97-108; Chapter 4 is abridged from *Hearing and Knowing* (ibid.): 109-19; Chapter 5 first appeared in *Stand Firm and Take Action: A Festschrift for Milan Opocensky on His 65th Birthday* (Geneva: World Alliance of Reformed Churches, 1996): 275-83; Chapter 6 is taken from Dale T. Irvin and Akintunde E. Akinade, eds., *The Agitated Mind of God: The Theology of Kosuke Koyama* (Maryknoll, N.Y.: Orbis Books, 1996): 201-11; Chapter 7 was first published in *Concilium* (25/6, 1989): 23-30; Chapter 8, abridged here, was first published in my *Daughters of Anowa: African Women and Patriarchy* (Maryknoll, N.Y.: Orbis Books, 1995): 1-16; Chapter 9, abridged here, is taken from the book I edited with Musimbi R. A. Kanyoro, *The Will to Arise: Women, Tradition, and the Church in Africa* (Maryknoll, N.Y.: Orbis Books, 1992): 152-171; Chapters 10 and 11, both abridged here are taken from *Daughters of Anowa* (ibid.): 172-87 and 208-18 respectively.

INTRODUCTION
The Girl called Amba Ewudziwa

The first memorable appearance I made at church was on a Palm Sunday. I was reading Matthew 21:1–11 in Mfantse, the version of Akan we speak at home. Papa, Charles Kwaw Yamoah, Methodist minister, was at his first ministerial posting at Akyenakrom near Kumasi. Mama, Mercy Dakwaa Yamoah, and the whole household were involved in this ministry. Papa was instilling a meticulous, almost stoic, way of life in the household. I had had to rehearse the passage with the right pauses and intonations until I could almost say it from memory, and of course, exactly as Papa would have it read. That is how public speaking began for me. I was not yet twelve but I was a Sunday School teacher and a chorister.

That Palm Sunday remains with me even after the innumerable occasions of participating in worship services. Of course, I do not remember my first appearance at church but 15 years ago my baptism certificate showed up telling me when I was born and that I was baptised in April 1934, still a baby. Now fast approaching seventy, I still count these two appearances as the beginning of my theological formation. Long before that, I had known that I was named on the eighth day of arrival on this planet as Amba Ewudziwa after my paternal grandfather, Kodwo Ewudzi Yamoah, 'Leader of the founders of the Methodist church at Asamankese'. I had known that I was born on his cocoa farm of Amoanna near Asamankese.

I cannot boast of being a first generation Christian, for both parents had grandparents who were Christian – Presbyterians (or rather Basel) and Methodists (or rather Wesleyan). I remember clearly the centenary of Methodism in Ghana in 1935, for that was when my picture of my paternal grandmother, Maame Martha Aba Awotwiwa Yamoah, as bead woman, was engraved on my consciousness.

My life has been one eventful journey of travel. I am told I travelled with my parents in the Fantse speaking areas of Ghana when Papa was a school teacher. We stayed at Asamankese (Akyem area) when Papa went off to Wesley College, Kumasi, to train for the pastoral ministry. Asamankese had been home to both parents because their parents migrated there. Papa's mother was from Apam and his father from Ekaumkrom. Mama's mother was from Amakom (now part of Kumasi) and her father from Techiman

(Brong Ahafo). We have lived in Sunyani, Wenchi, Winneba and Akropong near Kumasi. Formal education began for me in a Methodist Primary School that was run in what I can now identify as an old mission house, built on stilts with lots of sand on the ground in which we learnt to form the letters of the alphabet and to acquire numeracy. In those days, that is the mid-1930s, you began with sand, graduated to slate and chalk, then to pencil and paper, and then, oh what bliss, your first pot of ink and a pen with a nib. There was status in being seen with ink smudges on your hands and clothes.

I consider my schooling fairly uneventful. I moved through the ranks for ten years from class 1 to 3 and then standard 1 to 7. I wondered, even at that age, why some children had to be sent home for fees almost every month; why some missed classes and others were habitual latecomers; why some never seemed to be able to understand anything or even speak English. I spent my early school years moving, as my parents moved to Asamankese, Akyinakrom, Efiduase and then Kumasi. At Kumasi I began for the first time the privilege of being in 'elite' schools – Mmofraturo, Methodist Girls Boarding School, Achimota School, Kumasi College of Technology, now Kwame Nkrumah University of Science and Technology, the University of Ghana, Legon, Cambridge University, UK. I have also in my itinerant teaching career been associated with several prestigious names.

Teaching as a career has been challenging as well as most edifying. I began at a girls' school and in the five years had to think a lot about the education of girls, teenage pregnancy, early marriages, rumours of abortions and occasional drop-outs for no apparent reason. I met some of the girls I had taught as very successful traders in Kumasi market and others who were still unemployed but unable to further their education. What was the purpose of education? Was the Church doing it any differently from the government? Why was school not more skill-oriented? It was in fact a relief when, after a couple of years at another girls' school, the prestigious Wesley Girls High School, I was invited into an informal educational set up.

Moving from Ghana to Geneva, Switzerland, was not a big step. I had had two years of Cambridge, UK. I had been in the Students Christian Movement (SCM). While at Volta Hall, University of Ghana (1959–63), Joanna Lindsay and I had been catalysts in forming a prayer group around Cecilia Nwokolo, a Nigerian Law student who had a fracture and could not attend morning prayers. This group was later adopted by some British people who made it the basis for what became the Christian Union. I could not keep up with the demands of the group. I felt the traditional Christian creeds and the discipline of the Methodist Church were enough. At Achimota School, I had learnt the rudiments of ecumenism as all Protestants worshipped together. I did not feel the need for another group to guide my being saved. I needed a group to help me try to understand what it meant to live in the world as a Christian. It was SCM connections that got me to Geneva and SCM formed Modupe Oduyoye, the Nigerian SCM General Secretary, who became my spouse. I was elected president of the World Student Christian Federation from 1972 to 1976.

My ecumenical journey proper spans the years 1966 to date. My first ecumenical conference outside Ghana was at Bolden, Switzerland. The theme was 'Christian Education and Ecumenical Commitment'. This was followed by an Assembly in Nairobi, 1966, at which the World Sunday Schools Association merged with the World Council of Christian Education (WCCE). I was appointed jointly by the WCCE and the World Council of Churches (WCC) as Youth Education Secretary. This was part of the move to merge the WCCE into the WCC for the creation of a Department of Christian Education. I think it was at the WCC's Fourth Assembly at Uppsala that this merger was concluded.

Talking of Assemblies, I have been to every WCC Assembly since Uppsala. This is how it happened. At Uppsala, I was one of the eight-person Youth Department staff of the WCC. At Nairobi, I was one of the few specially invited women that the central committee of the WCC had agreed to persuade the member churches to bring as delegates so that there might be at least 12% women delegates. I was not just a presence. I co-moderated the standing committee on Dialogues with People of Other Faiths. I was nominated to the Central Committee and so went to Vancouver as returning Central Committee. I served on the Faith and Order Commission and later was on its standing commission until I went back on staff as a Deputy General Secretary. In this position I had responsibility for the Programme Guidelines Committee of the Canberra Assembly. At the last Assembly held in Harare, I found myself present as one of the persons being honoured for long-term association with the WCC but I was also there as a speaker at the Africa Forum. I was at the Decade Festival, which preceded the Assembly.

I had special relations with the Decade process having led the Bible study that mapped out the key issue for the Decade. I had written *Who Will Roll the Stone Away?* to sum up the first two years of the Decade, and had stayed close to the whole effort. I had been fully involved in the previous effort made under the rubric, 'Community of Women and Men in Church and Society'. Having organised the Africa Conference, I had the honour of presenting to the WCC Committee President the report of the concluding meeting held at Sheffield.

My sensitivity to the issues of gender began with moving from Ghana to Nigeria; trying to teach theology in a department where all my colleagues were men, and trying to understand the status of women in patrilineal Africa where some of us are matrilineal, I had to write *Daughters of Anowa*, as well as many other articles and chapters in books. It was this experience that led to my taking the initiative that resulted in the formation of the Circle of Concerned African Women Theologians in 1989. The Circle was preceded by efforts on my part to identify and recommend African women theologians to become members of the Ecumenical Association of Third World Theologians, of which I am the current president, with a five-year term that ends in October 2001. The Institute of African Women in Religion and Culture that I direct is in line with the

Circle's concern for women to tell their own stories and seek and safeguard their humanity.

The association with the Ecumenical Association of Third World Theologians (EATWOT) began with the EATWOT Africa Continental Conference held in Accra in 1977. For this conference I had offered a paper with the title, 'The importance of African traditional religious beliefs and practices for doing theology'.

While studying for the London University BD at the Department for the Study of Religions, University of Ghana, Legon, I had become keenly aware of the role primal religions around the world had played in bringing about the acceptance of religions that claim to transcend race and ethnicity, especially Christianity and Islam. I was deeply conscious of how thoroughly religious our traditional practices are. In addition, having read dogmatics and the development of Christian theology, I was aware of the critical nature of the battle for orthodoxy. In this regard, two books that have touched my imagination are in Cambridge University Press 'Studies in Church History' series, edited by G.J. Cuming and Derek Baker: the eighth volume, bearing the title, *Popular Belief and Practices*, and volume 9, *Schism, Heresy and Religious Protest*. They remind me of the struggle to shape orthodoxy, biblical and historical. I began to review the Christian history of Africa and the theological symbols that are most prevalent in popular preaching. I struggled to deal with them in my history and theology classes, in the SCM Senior Friends groups, as well as in the sermons in schools and women's Bible Studies that I was occasionally invited to lead. It was this experience that resulted in my first theological work, *Hearing and Knowing: Theological Reflections on Christianity in Africa*.

Hearing and Knowing was not my first book. My first book was a cartoon booklet entitled, *Youth Without Jobs*, and the second volume, *Flight from the Farms*. I still agonise over the former. And though living in a concrete wilderness in Accra, I try to farm. I even have four cocoa trees to remind me that I was born on my paternal grandfather's cocoa farm on a Saturday in October when the cocoa harvest was on. I have come to join the harvest. I was myself the 'first fruit' of my parents and in the theological world in Africa became the first fruit of the university's effort to blaze the trail of inclusiveness in all fields. A woman studying for an Honours degree in Theology, or even Religions, as it turned out to be, was a rarity. What is she going to become? A teacher, of course, I told all who enquired. With teaching came public speaking and writing. With theology came the passion for justice and dignity. With teaching came also all my involvements in humanisation and with this, an interest in the development of characters in African novels, especially those by women.

An autobiography is a select account of one's life. This selection is made so you might read the following chapters with some idea of who is speaking. There is, of course, a lot more about me. But I do not think you need to know that I take a walk every morning to ask nature to join me in praying, that I like the feel of the soil on my bare fingers...

I. Africa and Redemption

CHAPTER 1

Created and Redeemed

The exodus event

Reflection on the departure of the children of Israel from Egypt gives us valuable insight into the Judeo-Christian recognition of God at work and into theology generally. Creation and redemption, interwoven processes in which God is revealed, are seen by Christians following the Jewish heritage from the perspective of the exodus event. Dawn and light are often used as symbols of deliverance, thus bringing together creation and exodus (see Is. 8:20; 9:2; 33:2; Lam. 3:23; Jn. 8:12).

I begin with the exodus event, first because it is in harmony with my own experience. Second, it is the deliverance from Egypt that made possible the whole Hebrew experience as a people who were God's special creation. The exodus event explains and interprets their history. The victory song led by Miriam (Ex. 15) rings authentically and spontaneously – just what a group of Fante women would have done after a breathtaking deliverance.

> Sing to the Lord, for he has triumphed gloriously;
> because 'he is indeed very high' [*kiy ga'oh ga'ah*],
> ... the horse and his rider he has thrown into the sea. (Ex. 15:1).

Yahweh is indeed very high. As their history unfolded and the Hebrews began to recognise 'the hand of God' in their realities and to understand the depths of God's liberative works, the Song of Moses was composed. God is powerful, God is glorious, God wins victories. They understood this liberative activity as the outcome of the nature of God as a caring God.

God was present in the conquest of Canaan and in the building of the nation and its temple. Israel saw itself as uniquely God's and the experience of sealing the covenant at Mount Sinai sealed this faith. From then on, not just the community but individuals as well were believed to be unique in their relationship with Yahweh, and the affirmation is repeated throughout Scripture: 'The Lord is my strength and my song... my salvation' (Ps. 118:14).

Yahweh is a warrior who crushes the enemy in order to deliver the oppressed, who cry for liberation. Yahweh enables them to build in glory. Yahweh brings glory out of nothingness. The priestly theologians of the Jews set down their version of the creation myth of their part of the world in terms of chaos and its resolution. Within the creation narrative is embedded the Hebrew experience of deliverance. The meaning of life and of the world, for the community as well as for the individual, was to be found in the God who delivers. Faced with suffering and death, the people cry out and their cry goes up to God: 'Save, Oh Yahweh. He who delivered the children of Israel from Egypt, Daniel from the lions, and Jonah from the whale, why can't he deliver me?' Africans forcibly taken to the Americas and those left to labour at home for the same oppressors adopted the Christian faith and joined in the Hebrew affirmation that Yahweh triumphs over chaos. This affirmation was submerged when Paul 'spiritualised' the exodus (I Cor. 10:1–5). Redemption by Yahweh is limited to redemption from sin by Christ. The cry of the oppressed through the ages has often been either ignored or interpreted in terms of their personal sinfulness, thus letting-be the sinful structures that threaten to suffocate us all.

Our burden

In Africa, as we have seen, it is the experience of liberation from colonialism and the cry for this liberation that have stimulated theologies that struggle to be relevant to the realities of Africa. Indeed, in the political struggles that led to independence, the motif of the exodus from Egypt was a paradigm that played a key role as the charismatic leaders were cast in the image of Moses. In Ghana, the struggle was seen as a march out of colonialism that would set the people on the road to freedom. The party anthem of the ruling Convention People's Party was 'Lead, Kindly Light'. It was indeed a revolution; the Ga women expressed it as 'an about-face [that] has been shouted'. Turn your back on the fleshpots of Egypt and face the struggles of the desert. The slogan of the party – Freedom – was a cry and a hope. In Kenya, the leader of the Mau Mau changed his name to 'the light of Kenya', Jomo Kenyatta. Thus it is apposite to examine the theological content of the biblical exodus, to listen to what it has said and can say to Africa, as the nations struggle to be fully liberated from colonialism and from their internal misgoverning of themselves.

The traditional ordering of society placed its own burdens on the African people. So African theologians do not see the problem as one of captivity only to foreign nations. The task is not to retain and uphold tradition until the exile is over and a return and rebuilding can take place. In relation to traditional society one can still see the exodus as a paradigm, a departure from inflexibly ascribed positions whose hierarchical ordering was accepted as 'natural' and permanent. Notwithstanding the fact that almost everybody co-operated and deviants were punished, it was an oppressive system to the extent that to opt out was to be cast out.

The colonial period was not much different. White leadership was imposed (especially in urban areas) and colonial officers administered the country without involving the people, except for the few *akrakyefo* (clerks, civil servants) and *ahenfo* (traditional rulers) who were co-opted to see that the white man's bidding was done. The exodus was to get out of all this. Independent movements in Africa were not seen as a return to a pre-colonial order; rather they were a fresh chance for new things to happen. The hope was that these new things would bring about more humanisation; that is, bestow more dignity on the beings made in the image of God and called God's children.

Thus it was that the independent movements revived the recognition of charisma (placing it above birth) and applauded achievement (placing it above heritage) as the parameters by which to judge those assuming responsibility, especially as regards public office.[1] These leadership positions were not seen as permanent, and if 'the Spirit of God left you' and you ceased to seek the well-being and dignity of the people, you ceased to be a leader. With the emergence of a new elite under this principle of charismatic leadership, our perennial coups d'état were inaugurated. When charisma departs, despotism sets in and the people are moved to reject the person whom God had already rejected.[2]

Leaving the old behind

The exodus is a well-rehearsed event, and in Africa it has not grown stale. Just as the Jews retold it and relived it every time they were in need of, or were thankful for, deliverance, so do African Christians. It has become our story. It has ceased to be the exclusive story of the descendants of the Habiru and has become universally applicable to all peoples who believe in God the Creator, who saves from chaos. There follows a rereading of Exodus 1–3 (the situation of the Hebrews in Egypt) and Exodus 12:29–34 (the Tenth Plague) with special focus on the people who were caught up in a human predicament.

The *children of Israel,* an immigrant people, lived among the Egyptians. The leaders of Egypt began to feel threatened by their presence and took steps to curb their development. Under their new policy, the Hebrews were forced to build for others. Life became unbearable under the hard and alienating labour, but the Hebrew population still grew, as happens often under oppressive and dehumanising situations.

So the Egyptian authorities decided to control the Hebrew population by the most direct method: infanticide. Only females were to live, since if males were allowed to survive, they might join with invaders against the oppressive regime. The Hebrews groaned under the burden, and cried out to God (Ex. 2:23–25). A number of Egyptian and Hebrew women buried their ethnic allegiances and took the side of God to frustrate the efforts of Pharaoh and to promote life. Let's take a look at them.

The *midwives* were women who refused to be co-opted by the oppressor. The narrator says it is because they were God-fearing. They had skills which could be put to demonic use, but it seems they saw to the safe delivery even of Egyptian women. They must have been both compassionate and competent and were obviously full of wisdom.

Jochebed and Miriam were the mother and daughter who schemed day and night so that Moses might live. Their agony must have been beyond bounds. They, like the midwives, had to devise a way of getting around the oppressors' instructions. *Pharaoh's daughter* did exactly the opposite of what her father had decreed. She saved a Hebrew boy instead of destroying him. Miriam, the intelligent sister, dutifully watching her baby brother (a familiar African scene), was at hand to see that Moses was returned to his own mother.

Moses, the charismatic leader who emerged from this situation of oppression, alienation, and dehumanisation, began by treating Pharaoh with dignity; he talked to him as one who would heed the voice of God, one who would respond to God. Moses began with negotiation; he asked leave for the people to go on a retreat to meet their God. Instead of the situation getting better, it took a turn for the worse. The accredited leaders of the children of Israel (the taskmasters) took the side of the oppressors and agreed to carry on their assignment of making sure the Hebrews were economically productive. They must have suffered the dilemma of the co-opted, a situation well illustrated in Africa's colonial history. They had to weigh evil against evil and try to discover the lesser evil; they chose physical existence under inhuman conditions, to death. Perhaps they saw nothing to die for! The people too were ambivalent about their liberator, Moses, who claimed to be acting on the instructions of the God of their ancestors, Yahweh. When they experienced setbacks and obstacles on their way to freedom, they asked, 'Were there no graves in Egypt?' They too had nothing to die for, not even the name of God who comes to save. Life for these migrant people had been reduced to mere existence, and the courage to be the people of God had almost left them. Although they were landless, the promise of getting a homeland and becoming a people did not excite them, the fleshpots of Egypt were too attractive. They found it difficult to exchange a certain present for an uncertain future.

God does not rescue people in spite of themselves. The people had to be fully involved in their own liberation, women and men alike. Hence there appear in this story of liberation, villains, heroines, heroes, oppressors and oppressed, those whose orientation is toward the saving work of God and those who operate according to the power they wield as human beings.

Moses proved himself a leader even before he was called, attempting according to his light to bring reconciliation among the oppressed. Once a privileged member taken from the oppressed to enjoy the favours of the palace, he became the challenger of the authority of Pharaoh over the Hebrew people. He understood from his experience on Mount Sinai that the destiny of the children of Israel was to be servants of Yahweh, not of Pharaoh. He had earlier renounced the privileges of the elite in order to identify with the oppressed and had for a time been a refugee from Egyptian law. After his encounter on the mountain, he was to use the skills he had acquired by his education and vocation to confront the powers. But Moses could never have liberated the people without their co-operation. His credentials were questioned, not only by Pharaoh but also by his own people: 'Who made you a prince and a judge over us?' (Ex. 2:14).

Pharaoh's image is that of the oppressor. He is totally self-centred. He cannot see himself without the Hebrew slaves, portraying the psychology of those who say, 'I am because I dominate'.[3] The powerful never let go because they cannot exist as entities in themselves; they are nothing if they do not have others to trample under their feet or to look down upon. They know no other life and therefore have to do all they can to retain the situation that gives them their dominant role; hence they are dehumanised and they dehumanise others. In the exodus event as narrated, every round of negotiations resulted in further hardships for the oppressed. The powerful and dominant, like Pharaoh, only let go when they are directly affected by the calamities caused by their actions and decisions. It was only when Pharaoh lost his firstborn that he 'let go'. In the end, in trying to safeguard his way of life, he lost even his physical existence as an individual. The sufferings of the people he ruled, both natives and immigrants, did not move him; neither did the disharmony that afflicted the rest of creation in his domain.[4]

Pharaoh's action was motivated in his eyes by his desire to safeguard the security of his domain; he was being prudent. It was this political sagacity that dictated the policy to wear the Hebrews down with labour, to use their own people to subjugate them. Do everything to break their backs and their spirits. All this he commanded out of his fear of losing power and prestige. Oppressors are only fulfilled if there are others they can oppress. *Ohuruye ti mu mpa mmogya,* 'the tsetse fly must always have blood in its head, or it ceases to be a tsetse fly'.

Yahweh heard the crying and the groaning and called to mind (Ex. 6:5) the covenant made with Abraham, Isaac, and Jacob. God saw and knew the misery of the people (Ex. 2:23–25). Deliverance from Egypt was linked to the covenant – not only that covenant made with 'the ancestors' but also that covenant made with the people on Mount Sinai, which made all the people responsible for its keeping and beneficiaries of its blessings. But 'Who is Yahweh?' Moses, Pharaoh, the people – all asked this question.

The Yahwist narrator's answer is that Yahweh is El Shaddai, the fighting God, who is in a holy war against oppression from whatever quarter. Yahweh will use power to rout the oppressor (Ex. 6:23; 7:4). Yahweh's power is the power to save. In the exodus event, Israel experienced Yahweh's promise to make them a people, to give them land, and to be God to them. Yahweh becomes the reason for Israel's existence; they describe themselves by God, they are the people of God, not just the children of Abraham or Israel. It is God who makes their nationhood possible.

African Christian theologians, though operating from a religiously pluralistic context, claim that it is the same One God of all creation who operates in Africa as elsewhere and who is recognised in the religions of the continent.[5] Laying claim to the Jewish-Christian heritage of the exodus becomes a matter of faith in the One God, Creator and Liberator. The oppressed in the exodus story were immigrants; in Africa's history, it is the oppressor who is the immigrant, and in Africa oppression takes many forms.[6]

Multiple burdens

People live on their own soil in Africa, but are exploited by immigrants, as in a situation of colonialism. Others live on their own soil but are virtually working for overlords overseas. This situation of neo-colonialism exists throughout Africa, for planting coffee and cocoa is close to the forced labour of building pyramids. Oppressive situations are created by sheer self-seeking and love of power. There are those people who suffer under the above oppressions and are also treated as minors, whose manner of contributing is dictated by tradition, not aptitude or need.

These situations are the most alienating, because people come to accept what is said of them. They become strangers to their own potential and cannot imagine any other way of organising society or their personal lives. The norm of operation is that 'things-as-they-are' is the best way. This situation calls for *metanoia*, a hundred and eighty degree reorientation toward the person as the child of God and the whole people as the people of God.

Decoding the exodus

I cannot help but hear the promise and the call to the adventure of freedom in the exodus story. In every situation of alienation some escape the internalisation syndrome. They recognise that a situation that prevents one from full human responsibility cannot be natural. This realisation informs rebellion against the so-called normal, traditional, natural way. It stimulates the crying and the groaning. The individual Hebrew was liberated in order to get on the road to fulfilment. But the exodus is not so much personal as it is political. Pharaoh made a socio-political decision. His consideration had to do with cheap labour and state security; he neglected the fact that the personal growth and the well-being of both ethnic groups involved (Egyptian natives and Habiru immigrants) would be affected by his decision. When God saves, God saves totally. God purges the socio-political chaos in order to provide an atmosphere within which the fullness of humanity can flower.

We see also in the exodus story the various uses of power. Power in the sense of ability or authority to make things happen, or to prevent them from happening, may be said to be neutral. God's power in the exodus was creative: the power to save, to create space in which people could grow. But power can be put to negative use, and in the hands of Pharaoh it was. That kind of power is to be repudiated and broken. In the exodus we see also how God uses the skills and willingness of human beings and even their social status to bring about liberation – the daughter of Pharaoh, the midwives, the eloquence of Aaron, and the long association of Moses with the court of Pharaoh.

In Africa, human initiatives in the liberation process are acknowledged. The charismatic leaders are recognised as God-sent and the people put their hands in theirs. The pioneer leaders were treated as God's gift to the suffering people. In some parts of Africa, the process of political liberation was conceived and described in religious terms. Most conspicuous was Kwame Nkrumah's Convention People's Party (CPP) with its anthem 'Lead, Kindly Light'. God was seen as being in the situation because the situation was liberative. Foreign rule was to be overthrown in order to enable Africans to build up a new society. Critics were to denounce this combination of the political and the religious as blasphemous. Certain interpretations of the Young Pioneer Movement led to uneasiness that Ghana might be putting Nkrumah in the place of God, or at least that Nkrumah had embarked upon his apotheosis.[7] This does no more than illustrate the interpretation of the process of colonial liberation as a religious experience. Neither a Christian church closely associated with the foreign government nor the co-opted educated elite could be trusted. Like Pharaoh's taskmasters, both were identified with the oppressive regime.

When Nkrumah's statue was erected, it bore one of his supposedly blasphemous utterances: 'Seek ye first the political kingdom and everything else will be added'. Is the 'political kingdom' always opposed to the 'kingdom of God'? In the political kingdom that Ghana sought, the first were to be the last and the people were to express their wishes through the Party organisation right from village level. Another 'religious' aspect of the movement was that it was seen as a march: a people going in the wrong direction had turned around, led by the warrior whom God had sent, but above all, led by the Light of God. God had sent a Moses to get us out from under the burdens of colonialism and to make us a free nation with new opportunities for a fuller life. The exodus event is read as a call to freedom; it is the beginning of a process, just as the independence celebrations and the five-year development plans of Ghana are a call to the future.

Where church leaders read the independence struggle as a work of God, Christians had no problems with reconciling nationalism with Christianity. But in some places the missionaries, both black and white, read and reread Romans 13 to their congregations without any reference to Revelation 13. Only the status quo was seen as showing God's presence. Initially, the leaders of the independence movements were seen as troublemakers. They opened the eyes of people to the realities in their situations. But the leaders who confused the call to the desert with the possession of the promised land were bound to bring disillusionment to the people.

The exodus happened, the motley group of Habiru was changed into a nation under the hand of God. New life and new perspectives are possible if God is in the situation. The conclusion of the anti-independence missionaries was to refuse to see God working through the human agency that emerged among Africans. Whether one looks at the present politico-economic instability or repression of African countries from the perspective of neo-colonialism or that of exploitation by nationals, Africans have tasted liberation and are aware of the need to strive through the desert, through a state of continuing liberation from one oppressor or another. Whether Africans need new skills for running the courts of justice or new methods of economic survival, or even wars with the forces that prevent entry into the promised land, the sea has already been crossed.

The exodus event, attested to outside Hebrew literature, is a gift to the oppressed.[8] The meaning Israel found in this episode has been appropriated and reapplied by others in similar situations. Those who have known no socio-political and economic colonisation can afford the luxury of spiritualising the event. That too is legitimate if one can learn the meaning of sin and the implications of personal involvement in communal sin.

When oppressed peoples meet obstacles, the event of the exodus reassures them. Every triumph on the way evokes the Song of Miriam. Thus the journey to the promised land is a journey undertaken in the spirit of doxology. The oppressed become a people empowered by the presence of God-with-them and like Miriam they continually recognise God as the author of their success. The religious base of life in Africa enables us to read our history as 'sacred' history. *Gye Nyame*, 'Except God', is one of the pillars of the primal religion of the Ghanaian, for without God nothing holds together.[9] God intervenes here and now, making salvation and liberation one activity of God. We believe in providence and therefore are ready to see God in daily happenings, whether they concern the individual or the community.

Footnotes

[1] This is not entirely alien to the primal world-view of certain parts of Africa. The Igbo of Nigeria, for instance, lay great store by personal achievement. Achebe, Chinua, *Things Fall Apart* (Greenwich, Conn.: Fawcett, 1959).

[2] Although traditional rulers are never deposed for any reason whatsoever in some parts of Africa, in other parts this is always a possibility, as the rulers are constitutional monarchs. One cannot of course limit the impetus for the incessant coups d'état in Africa to this view of government alone.

[3] Zoe-Obianga, Rose, 'Resources in the Tradition for Renewal of Community', in C.F. Parvey, *The Community of Women and Men in the Church* (Geneva: World Council of Churches, 1983), 72; Taylor, J.V., *The Primal Vision: Christian Presence amid African Religion* (London: SCM; Philadelphia: Fortress Press, 1963), 85.

[4] Croatto, J. Severino, *Exodus: Hermeneutics of Freedom* (Maryknoll, NY: Orbis Books, 1981), 23–24.

[5] Pobee, John S., 'Church and State in Ghana', in John S. Pobee (ed.), *Religion in a Pluralistic Society* (Leiden: E.J. Brill, 1976), 129–42.

[6] Whatever the arguments as to the settling of South Africa, it is clear that whites came from another continent and that blacks belong to the African continent. The philosophy that 'occupation is nine-tenths of the law' cannot be allowed to go unchallenged.

[7] God's rule through human agencies – including political parties, parliaments, and presidents – operates only as they recognise God as the true ruler and themselves as stewards. Hence the cautions of Revelation 13:18 and the call for wisdom.

[8] Attestation of Hebrew antiquities aided by archaeology has enhanced our understanding of the exodus and the settlement of Palestine. See comments by Alexander Jones, general editor of *The Jerusalem Bible* (New York: Doubleday, 1966), 10–11.

[9] *Gye Nyame* is troublesome to translate, as none of the English equivalents bring out the nuance of, 'Without God all falls apart, returns to nothingness, becomes meaningless, yields no fruits, does not succeed'. In Ghana, 'Except God' has become the accepted English formula.

CHAPTER 2

Except God

_____

Creation As Liberation

Without God nothing holds together; nothing has any meaning. It is God, *Bɔrebɔre*, who fashioned the universe (*bɔ adze*), who called Being into being.[1] To read Genesis 1 is to call to mind the universal intuition that the universe, all in it and all that happens in it, has a Designer and Maker. 'Things' are not here by chance, and one expects an answer to the call, 'Is anyone in charge here?' In Genesis, God 'delivers' the universe from chaos, just as out of compassion God delivered the Habiru from Egypt. The narrative does not pretend to be a history of origins or a scientific explanation of what is. It is an attempt to say who God is, to affirm that chaos is contrary to the nature of God, and that the universe came into being out of the 'pain of God'.

In the creation stories of the Mesopotamian civilisation, Marduk (the Good Force) rescues the world from the belly of Tiamat (the dragon, the Evil Force), or uses her body as material for making the heavens and the earth. The Hebrew narrative is one of several such stories that were told in eastern Mediterranean lands.[2] The Hebrew version is unique in that it tells of God's transforming a chaotic situation by a creative act that rescued the 'earth' from formlessness – *Tohu wa Bohu*, 'emptiness and formlessness'. This is how the priestly theologian of Genesis 1 perceives God. Creation was a deliberate act of God, who acted freely to bring meaning to what otherwise would have been 'tractless waste and emptiness'.[3] Out of the darkness over the deep comes an orderly succession of light and dark. Yahweh was totally in control, and in a neat six-day operation all was complete and God could rest; the universe had been given a (new) beginning and the earth began its individual existence in the context of God's ordered creation.

The second narrative (Gen. 2:4–25) puts more 'matter' into the event. The earth-creature is made from earth, and the serpent sets itself up to oppose Yahweh like a dragon from the Mesopotamian myths. As in those narratives, the serpent caused humanity's mortality. (In the myth, the herb of rejuvenation given to Gilgamesh by Uta-Napishtim was devoured by the serpent who left his old skin behind).[4] Several biblical references echo the Mesopotamian stories in which God steps into a situation to redeem matter from formlessness. Marduk struggled to make the good heaven and the good earth out of the body of the evil Tiamat, but the Hebrew Yahweh of the priestly view simply calls into being, transforms non-existence into existence. The Yahwist writer preserves bits of the primeval struggle found in other versions.

The history of the Jews is the paradigm of transformation. In their collective memory and national experience, God transformed a heterogeneous group of individuals and tribes into a nation under God by the Sinai covenant. This transformation is repeated in the lives of individuals who cry to God.[5] Similarly, an Akan folktale tells of Ananse Kokroko (the Great Spider, a linguistic device employed to avoid using God's personal name, Nyame), who was aware of constant fighting between 'Half and Half'. Ananse Kokroko steps in, gets hold of the two, slams them together, and out of two made one whole human being. This is one of the few creation stories the Akan have; in it we see God's direct involvement in order to transform a situation of disharmony.

According to the elaborate creation myth of the Yoruba, Olódùmàre fashioned the earth and all that it contains through the use of agents, but closely supervised the process personally. By whatever process, when humans think of their earthly home, they perceive God at work. I do not know of any primal world-view of Africa that leaves our existence to chance. God is at work making a new thing out of the chaotic old. It is interesting to note that during the Habiru's days in the desert, even the serpent was transformed into a salvific agent (Num. 21:9; Jn. 3:14).

The creation story of Genesis 1 is about the redemption that God brings to our chaotic world. It is a theological statement affirming that God responds to situations. God, as the Hebrew and the Akan perceive, is not the Impassible One of Greek philosophy. God is affected and is not immune to mutability. In fact, God is plainly vulnerable. It is this co-passionate (compassionate) and 'vulnerable' God that Christians see in Christ. God so loved that God sent. John 3:16 tells of the suffering love of God; the same love that conquered chaos pities the human condition and sends help. God so suffered with our suffering humanity and our suffering world, that God did something about the situation: 'While we were yet afar off ... God looked out for us' (Lk. 15:20). God turned in our direction: 'As a father pities his son, so the Lord pities those who fear him' (Ps. 103:13).[6] One of the unique contributions of Christianity to religion is the doctrine that the Messiah who suffered is certainly the very image of the suffering God. God's creative and redemptive powers flow out of this suffering love.

In the creation narratives, one may trace the theme of redemption/liberation/salvation in Genesis 2–3. To correct the state of alone-ness and to create a community, God makes two sexes out of the earth-creature, Adam.[7] Even when mistrust leads human beings to take their destiny into their own hands and to attempt to do without God, God still has compassion, cares and provides 'a covering' for the shame-evoking nakedness of the woman and the man.

Among the Igbo of Nigeria, to be creative is to turn the power of evil, sin and suffering into the power of love. When things are not going well in a community, in order to restore harmony and mutuality of existence, this African community requires artists to camp together, to work together to heal the society by their sacrifice. The creativity of the artists is the sacrifice required for righting wrongs in the community. The artists fashion a model of a whole community and all that they have in a house (*Mbari*), and the house and its artifacts are left as a sacrifice, which will renew the community. (For the Kikuyu of Kenya, the word *Mbari* means 'clan').[8] The artist symbolically recreates the clan in its pristine state through artifacts and the result is salutary for the real clan. It becomes once again a wholesome people in a wholesome community. This symbolic 'new creation' out of a chaotic old appears in the Bible in the stories of the flood, the replenishing of the world and the apocalyptic new creation of Revelation: 'Behold, I make all things new' (Rev. 21:5). Christianity believes this new creation has already begun with the coming of the Christ.

Owner of the earth

The creation narrative underlines the fact that the universe belongs to God who created it and that there is an interdependence of God's world and God's people. The story is a challenge and a judgement on how we run the world in our day. God speaks to humanity and humanity has the ability to respond to God. Made in God's image, we are expected to be God-like.

From this perspective we hear the narrator telling of the existing disharmonies of our world: disharmony in nature, caused by human excesses and irresponsibility (Gen. 3,4,6). To tell this tale of woe, the narrator begins with a scene in which God is 'absent' (Gen. 3:1–7). The woman talks about God with the serpent (the opponent of God); the man stands by, not taking part in this theological disputation, but also completely forgetful of his responsibility to God who had commanded that the fruit of that tree was not to be eaten. The woman, restating and interpreting God's command, puts the case even stronger than God had, adding that the tree must not even be touched. 'You shall not eat of the fruit of the tree .... neither shall you touch it, lest you die' (Gen. 3:3). This is a rabbinic device called hedging the Torah. But knowing the law does not necessitate obedience.[9] An analysis of God's intentions begun, the woman proceeded to look to what she thought was her self-interest. She came to the conclusion that the reason for keeping away from the tree was simply obedience to God. But why obey? She decided to experiment and persuaded the man, the unquestioning collaborator, who acquiesced to the demands of another, who claimed to have thought through the whole issue and weighed all its aspects.

The narrator, looking at his own society and perceiving various levels of disintegration and disharmony, tells this persuasive and 'true' story: we do make a mess of our world when we ignore God's voice and mis-use both the natural order and our human companions in the process of seeking our interests. The earth is the Lord's, not ours, and hence there is a limit to how far we can bend it to suit ourselves. Contravening the laws that hold it together cannot but result in a return to the chaos from which it was created. The cynicism of the snake, the distrust of the woman and the apathy of the man, are all well-known elements in the generation and maintenance of chaos in the context of the world within which the story was being told as they are in ours today.

Nevertheless, the redemptive effort is continued as the woman continues to work in today's world for the mutuality decreed by God and denied by the man. The male principle in the world, however, instead of seeking community, attempts to forestall being an unquestioning follower by swinging to the other end of the pendulum and becoming a being whose power to be depends on the non-being of others. Neither domination nor acquiescence in human relations can make for a healthy community. Only participation will do it; hence the emphasis on *Koinonia* in the Christian community. The Hebrew narrator, being a man of his time, puts into the mouth of God words that validate the status quo, stating them as if God were decreeing what ought to be, rather than stating what becomes inevitable when we refuse to live *coram Deo*. In the scene that tells of the consequences of disobedience (Gen. 3:14–19), God is present.

When God returned, cynicism, distrust, and apathy were declared illogical in the divine-human relationship. Far from sanctioning our evil ordering of society, this myth is a judgement on our refusal to observe limits, an outcome of the yearning to be independent of God. To be totally dependent on God, we have to have absolute trust in God. The Hebrew answer to the question, 'Is there any one in charge here?' is, 'Yes!' God is in charge and God gives us what is for our good. Cynicism in our relationship to God cannot make for a healthy human community. Our community with God depends on our complete trust in God. We experience a chaotic world of human creation, ecological disruption, and the absence of *Shalom* – the groaning of the whole creation (Rom. 8:22–23). By magic, science and technology, we claim the 'right' to use and misuse the earth, assuming that it is humanity that is in charge here.

In Africa, as elsewhere, a literal reading of the creation narratives has stifled the theological content and buried the chance for real reflection. A re-reading of Genesis 1–3 from the perspective of the liberated children of Israel conveys other messages. The narrative, far from sanctioning what is, is a judgement on the world as we run it. It exposes the sin in patriarchy as well as that in matriarchy. Hierarchy that undermines community and ignores individuals' ability to contribute, is condemned. The story exposes our refusal to observe limits set by the God who frees from chaos and who is the only lawgiver. We would gladly put limits on others if that made us feel fulfilled, and yet to have dominion over the earth involves being disciplined. The narrative shows our unbelief in our verbal acknowledgement that God knows what we need. It calls us back to God in our original shameless nakedness, vulnerability and mutuality. It calls for mutual respect, respect for the toughness and tenderness that is latent or patent in both women and men. Above all, the narrative talks of the love of God for a recalcitrant world.

The theme of love that goes to the rescue is illustrated throughout the gospels in stories of healing and teaching, which present us with a God who suffers to give us the chance of a second birth. Saving us from ourselves, God effects our exodus, thus beginning our re-creation. Our problem is that we are not sheep, but moral agents, able to say, 'No', to God. So neither wins and God bears the burden of waiting longingly for us: 'Behold, I stand at the door and knock' (Rev. 3:20). 'I will take you for my people, and I will be your God' (Ex. 6:7). 'You shall remember that you were a slave in Egypt' (Deut. 16:12). More than this, God actually searches for us and suffers until the community is complete.

A theology divorced from ethical demands would have little relevance in Africa. The exodus theme in Africa poses not only a question of liberation but one of, 'What shall we *do* to be saved?' For we shall not live the lives of a people of God if we only say, 'Lord, Lord', and we do not do what the Lord tells us (Lk. 6:46). It is to highlight the necessity for an ethic of a redeemed people that African theologians need to review christology. When this has been done, it will become clearer what it means to say: 'Believe in the Lord Jesus, and you will be saved, you and your household' (Acts 16:31). The word that needs to be heard on this continent is the plan to redeem all that has been created by God. Salvation for an elite who have no responsibility to the community at large, is contrary to the meaning of the Christ-event. For it is the One God without whom there is no existence, who has accomplished our salvation in Christ.

Footnotes

1 *Bɔrebɔre* is a praise-name that signifies God's creative activity. Oduyoye, Modupe, *The Sons of the Gods and the Daughters of Men* (Maryknoll, NY: Orbis Books, 1984), relates this Fante word to the Hebrew '*bowre*', 'creator'.

2 Shapiro, Max S. and Rhoda A. Hendricks, *A Dictionary of Mythologies* (London: Granada, 1981), xxi, 119.

3 *The Jerusalem Bible* (New York: Doubleday, 1966), 15.

4 Parrott, André, *Noah's Ark* (London: SCM, 1955), 9, gives what is no doubt an etiological story. It is of interest because the python features in not a few stories of 'beginnings' in Africa.

5 Gottwald, Norman K., *The Tribes of Yahweh: A Sociology of the Religion of Liberated Israel 1250–1050 BCE* (Maryknoll, NY: Orbis Books, 1979), xxiii, 'Moses', 35–40, 'Religious Idealism', 592–607, and 'The "uniqueness" of Israel', 672–75.

6 *Racham* as used here could have been translated as 'love' – hence my recalling Psalm 103 and John 3:16. On a continent being shaped by Christianity and Islam, *Racham* becomes even more crucial in our theology, for 'compassion', one of the ninety-nine 'beautiful names' of God, is of the same Semitic root.

7 *Adam*, from *adamah*, 'earth-soil', leads to this rendition of the first human being (first adam) as a sexually undifferentiated being. See Gottwald, Norman K., *The Tribes of Yahweh,* 796–97, n. 628, for comments on Genesis 1:26–27.

8 Desai, Ram (ed.), *Christianity in Africa as Seen by Africans* (Denver: Allan Swallow, 1962), 101.

9 The apostle Paul's keen analysis of the human situation in this regard is apposite here. See also Romans 7, especially verses 22 and 23, noting that Paul is talking of what he has seen in his own life.

CHAPTER 3

Jesus Saves

The religious background to these studies is the primal religion of Africa and of Judaism. What we in Africa have traditionally believed of God and the transcendent order has shaped our Christianity. But that is only part of the story. Islam strides shoulder to shoulder with Christianity in Africa; the relationship of the two calls for serious consideration. Religious maturity, traditional hospitality to the stranger and the sacredness of blood ties, have enabled the adherents of these two faiths to accept the other's right to exist and in the family context to share each other's festivals. A practical dialogue has been initiated and goes on steadily. Nevertheless, a situation of uneasy peace is sometimes made volatile by the extremist elements on both sides. Theological dialogue has so far taken the form of two parallel monologues.

In such a situation, one needs to discover approaches to christology that will compel even those who claim to be without religion to pause and consider the Christ. The Christ in the popular theology of Africa is above all the one who saves. The slogan or affirmation, 'Jesus saves', is written large on the minds and hearts of African Christians, and in Nigeria, literally written on buttons, on cars and walls. What does it mean, what does it imply? The answer to this question should be the christological quest of our times. Proclaiming the divinity of Christ is in the dimension of faith, but his lordship over life is clear from the style of life he lived. His total dependence upon God's power and love demands that one give that style of life a trial as being the perfect salvific life.[1] What are the salvific implications of his death and resurrection, especially in the context of Islam? What does his humanity mean in view of sexism and racism? These are the questions I bring to christology.

Salvation and liberation

The *Agyenkwa*, the one who rescues, who holds your life in safety, takes you out of a life-denying situation and places you in a life-affirming one. The Rescuer plucks you from a dehumanising ambience and places you in a position where you can grow toward authentic humanity. The *Agyenkwa* gives you back your life in all its wholeness and fullness.

Who needs a Saviour?

Research into the phenomenon of religious conversion in Africa shows evidence of both spiritual and material struggles that prompted people to adopt Christianity. Those two struggles cannot be divorced one from the other. Our worship of nature and our refusal to examine what we call natural, the selective beneficence implied in ethnic morality, our confusion of pluralism with sectionalism, our worship of elitism and neglect of people's participation, our refusal to deal with corruptive influences and practices, our worship of patriarchy and hierarchy – these should make all of us seekers after salvation. It is apposite to observe therefore that cries for salvation in the Old Testament mirror cries from the African continent. Even a word-study approach to the faith will illustrate this.

If one studies the Old Testament with the knowledge of the primal world-view of Africa and an awareness of the political and sociological realities that are shaping Africa as part of one's critical equipment, many similarities surface. The primal cry for salvation (*yeshuah*) is taken up in the New Testament and salvation is declared by Christianity to be in Christ.[2] This, I believe, is the reason for the continued attractiveness of Christianity to Africans, in spite of the negative burdens associated with its carriers. The Christ of Christianity touches human needs at all levels, and Africans are but ordinary members of the human race feeling the need for salvation. I choose only two of the felt needs that show Africa's readiness to accept salvation through Jesus Christ as Saviour and Redeemer.

The Warrior-Saviour of the Hebrew Scriptures

Yahweh, who fought Israel's battles against human enemies, was called Yahweh Sabaoth, the commander of the large array of forces. In Asante military terminology, Yahweh would have been called the *Tufohene*, the one who manages the logistics of the military, both physically and spiritually, and who actually directs the battles, fighting alongside his people. When the Israelites called God by the praise-name Sabaoth, they were referring to actual experiences of 'God-at-war'. God, the Saviour from the rigours of battle, was a reality containing and eliminating actual enemies in literal battles. The salvation (Hebrew root word *Yasha*) wrought by God was felt immediately in military and political terms.

In the narratives dealing with the conquest of Canaan, no victory was won without God. When the Philistines molested the Israelites, they called upon Yahweh to save them (I Sam. 7). Yahweh was, in the experience of Israel, the One who gives victory. In the language of the Akan, a people that had experienced long years of ethnic conflicts, *Osagyefo*, the one who saves in the battle, became a praise-name of God. Hence also the Fante (Christian) lyrics that give God the praise-name *Osabarima*, the Great Warrior, the Lord of the Battle, literally, the Man of War. *Dɔmkuyin* in the song below is the best word to express Yahweh's praise-name, Sabaoth.

> *Wɔmfa ndaase mma hɛn Hene o*
> *Wɔmfa ntonton mma Dɔmkuyin*
> *Waadan hɛn* hell *ato hɛn* heaven *o*
> *Ɔsabarima e*
> *Yɛdawo ase a ɔsa o.*

> Bring thanks to our King.
> Bring praise to the Brave General
> Who has turned our hell to heaven.
> Saviour of the Battle
> We cannot thank you enough.

In the Christian lyrics, however, the spiritualisation of life's battles is already in evidence. We bring thanks to God who has led our feet from the path that leads to hell onto that which leads to heaven. In the same lyric, God is described as our Great Friend (*Adamfo Adu*) and Guarantor (*Okyirtaafo*). But even in this, one can see faith expressed in the God who transforms the experience of 'hell' as the Christians had known it into 'heaven' as they were beginning to experience it in the transformation of their primal and innate faith in God. The fact remains, nevertheless, and carries conviction for the African, that it is Yahweh who promises through Isaiah: 'I will contend with those who contend with you' (Is. 49:25). It is Yahweh who will smite the ruthless and the wicked (Is. 11:3–5).

Salvation as the overcoming of external physical enemies in war does not preclude the inner battle against evil inclinations. For, as Paul was to say later, the battle must be waged against the unseen powers (Eph. 6:10–20). The fact that all human beings need the salvation of God from these powers does not prevent God from saving those who need salvation on both scores, for Yahweh Sabaoth liberates all who cry to him (Is. 19:16–25). This is a remarkable view of God, showing that 'exodus' does not belong to only one nation or people called Israel. 'When they cry to the Lord because of oppressors he will send them a Saviour, and will defend and deliver them' (Is. 19:20).[3]

Our reconciliation

In Yahweh all peoples will be reconciled because they will all come under one rule, that of Yahweh. The salvation that Christ brought is in line with this, for not only does he unite us all in himself, but also in him we are at one with God.

This ministry of reconciliation to and in God is a key Christian interpretation of the Christ-event within Jewish-Christian salvation history. Jesus, in the Christian understanding, is the Christ, God's own 'chosen instrument for our salvation'. The name he bears, Jesus, is the hellenised version of the Hebrew name, Yeshuah (Joshua), but the situation he was sent to respond to, contained elements beyond those of the period of the conquest associated with his namesake of the Hebrew Scriptures. Israel was a conquered nation living in captivity, not in Egypt, Assyria, or Babylon, but right in the very land God gave it. Israel had fallen under Roman colonial rule; the people were free to worship Yahweh and keep the Law as long as neither conflicted with Roman rule. In the midst of political and social oppression, we cannot forget that on the personal level individuals may still be plagued by feelings of estrangement from God. When large issues of national economy are being considered, it is often the case that the welfare of people as persons becomes obscured.

The debate over whether Jesus forgave sins before healing physical ills or vice versa exists because we create a dichotomy between the elements of human well-being. The human being is still an integrated person in Africa, the private and the political cannot be separated. Jesus exposed the structures of oppression that operated from temple and synagogue, those inherent in the interpretations of the Law of God and of what it means to be a people of God. Jesus worked for the soundness of persons and structures, both religious and social.

Just as in the Hebrew Scriptures, Yahweh rescued people from childlessness and disease, famine and fire, from flood and from the deep sea, from disgrace and humiliation, so we find Jesus in the New Testament snatching women and men away from all domination, even from the jaws of death. He redeems by a strong hand all who are in the bondage of sin and who manifest their being in the service of sin by exploiting their neighbours. 'Today salvation has come to this house,' Jesus told Zacchaeus (Lk. 19:1–10), after a speech that echoes John the Baptist's preaching on the imminence of the Kingdom of God.

The One who redeems us

The images of the Warrior and of the Liberator are companion images; they give us hope for space in which to be truly human. The Liberator will set us free through the process of redemption. The imagery of God in Christ as Redeemer is one that speaks clearly to Africa. In primal societies the *pɔnfo*, the one who pays back a loan for someone in debt, is appreciated and revered. 'Redeeming' is also experienced through the custom of shaving off the hair of the widow and children at the death of husband and father. If they wish to keep their hair they have to 'buy it back' by paying a sum of money. Surely for those who do not want to be shorn, the one who enables them or allows them to 'redeem' their hair shows them sympathy and consideration. In several Fante hymns the 'Great Redeemer' (Jesus Christ) is called *Pɔnfo Kɛse* (see Lev. 25:47–50). Christians see themselves as having been taken away from the slavery of a lifestyle that was painful to God, to one that makes them the family of God.

In the early period of evangelisation in Africa south of the Sahara, which also coincided with the dying days of the slave trade, African Christians experienced redemption in its most literal form and therefore gave their lives to Christ. 'To redeem', then, is as much an African concept as it is a Jewish one. Africans passing into Christianity are bound to carry with them these primal connotations.

Liberating Israel from slavery in Egypt was a salvific act born out of God's grace (Ex. 15:13). This is what makes the historic exodus so fascinating. It is clear from that political deliverance that the redemption of a community from unjust systems is not outside God's providence, that what God found necessary to do for Israel, God has found necessary to do for the colonised peoples of Africa, and is doing for those held in bondage inside Africa.

This, however, is not the whole content of the rich store of redemption imagery in the Old Testament. Africa experiences realities from which nations and individuals daily cry to be redeemed. Some of these are like the experience of God's people, Israel.

Salvation discussions that focus exclusively on giving satisfaction (*mpata*) to the injured honour of God and on redemption by the blood of Christ, tend to lead to debates that leave the sinner and the slave as spectators.[4] Moreover, to redeem is not only to buy back. The marketplace terminology associated with redemption is not to be allowed to overshadow God's action of taking off our chains so that we may be free to be fully human. God snatches us away, separates us from the oppressive environment, breaks off unjust relationships and tears down dehumanising structures (Ps. 35:17; 136:24; Dan. 6:27–28).

To attempt a comprehensive survey of the situation from which people are redeemed by God is not possible here. Neither can I refer to the rich images and vocabulary of deliverance in the Hebrew Scriptures. I suggest a few in a summary fashion only:

- Deliverance of nation from nation (Jer. 31:11; Mich. 4:10; 2 Sam. 7:23)
- Deliverance from national sin (Ps. 44:26; 130:8)
- Deliverance of individuals from other people(s) (2 Sam. 4:9)
- Deliverance from dehumanisation (Job 5:15; Is. 45:15, 21; Ps. 72:2), from the poverty that makes people sell themselves to others
- Deliverance from personal actions that cause disrupture in the relations with others and with God (Ps. 51)
- God provides events to turn back to right religion those who have been lured into idolatry (2 Kgs. 10:18–27).

'Deliver us, liberate us and make a new nation of us; renew our humanity after the pattern inherent in you.' Redemption often includes the sense of rescue (*Yasha*). God gives safety by rescuing the bankrupt from the hands of the violent (Job 5:15). God rescues from death, from murderers and persecutors, from all evil. God saves the fugitive (and there are many refugees in and from Africa). In wartime, God rescues (*Padah*) from the stroke of the sword; God rescues from all troubles (Job 5:8–16).

Psalm 72 carries the message of peace that God defends the poorest and saves the children of those in need. God rescues from the hands of the greedy and callous sheep, and will judge between sheep and sheep. So Ezekiel warns the fat sheep who, not content to graze in good pastures, trample down the rest (34:17–22). To bring renewed vigour to the nation, God would rescue the nation from defilement and from the worship of idols, giving a new heart and a new spirit to all.

The redemption Africa experiences by turning to God through Christ is not only from 'wrong religion' and 'wrong government', it is also from the perversions of human nature that make it possible for some to prey on others and for individuals to trample upon the humanity of others.

God is concerned for the wholeness of our *be*-ing and for our relationship to God and to other human beings. 'Against thee, thee only, have I sinned,' said David after the scheming that resulted in Uriah's death and David's marriage to Bathsheba, Uriah's widow (Ps. 51:4). God's salvation is not only open to all. It is sufficient to cover the sin of all epochs of history.

The continuity of God's action in history has to be recognised if we are not to create Yahweh in the image of our own particular age. Here I wish to refer to a crucial factor underlying the understanding of salvation in the Hebrew Scriptures. The 'remember you were a slave in Egypt' memory of our own salvation should make us champions of the principles of the rule of God.

> It was not because you were more in number than any other people that the Lord set his love upon you and chose you, for you were the fewest of all peoples; but it is because the Lord loves you, and is keeping the oath which he swore to your fathers, that the Lord has brought you out with his mighty hand, and redeemed you from the house of bondage, from the hand of Pharaoh king of Egypt. (Deut. 7:7–8)

Our salvation is absolutely undeserved. God heard our cry, saw our discomfiture, saw us distraught under our oppressors, and liberated us. This liberation is for a purpose; it is in the plan of God to make us truly human. Therefore the memory of our being a redeemed people ought to make us obey injunctions laid on us.

> You shall not pervert the justice due to the sojourner or to the fatherless, or take a widow's garment in pledge; but you shall remember that you were a

slave in Egypt and the Lord your God redeemed you from there; therefore
I command you to do this. (Deut. 24:18)

Jesus the Saviour

The theme of idolatry was at the centre of early Christian preaching when
the early evangelists launched out into the Roman Empire. Records from the
New Testament, the early Fathers and Christian preaching in Africa, show
that this theme has never been ignored (see Tertullian, *De Nationes* and
Athanasius, *Contra Gentes*). But to confine idolatry to the divinities of the
primal religions allows us to ignore the worship of our modern idols, just as
limiting the meaning of slavery to the physical sale of persons allows our
modern exploitative systems to go uncriticised. Does Paul not equate greed
with idolatry (Col. 3:5–6)? Greed and other human failings can lead to our
being alienated from God and are indeed signs of our de facto refusal to
recognise the rule of God in human affairs.

No reading of the tasks that Jesus performed can fail to touch our life in
Africa – as persons, nations, and as a continent. Hence the prominent use of
Luke 4:18–22, the 'Manifesto' of Nazareth, and of Mary's Song of Revolution, the Magnificat (Lk. 1:46–55). People literally blind and in chains are
added to the numbers of those blind to the demands of the Kingdom of God
and chained by the desire to seek their own interests as if there is no power
beyond the human will. God, in sending Christ, has demonstrated the limited
power of physical discomfort. He has asked us not to accept physical pain
fatalistically, but with the power given us, to put an end to it. In Jesus, God
brings to us a style of life that puts others first, that saves others, leaving God
to bring about the resurrection that will transform one's own wretchedness.
Christ does not call us to use the teaching of dependence upon God to
domesticate or 'soften people for the kill', as some have accused Christianity
of doing.[5] On the contrary, while he demands that we turn the other cheek,
and pray for our persecutors as he did himself, he gives the example of refus-
ing to stand by while *others* are being hurt, exploited, cheated, or left to die.

In the New Testament, the battle against political oppression does not
loom large, but that should not blind us to its presence. Jesus did not take the
dramatic approach that some of his contemporaries would have liked. He had
a more radical answer: he put forward a world-view that eventually brought
down the Roman Empire and that has the dynamism to break down our
modern institutions that are geared toward the fulfilment of a few – if only
we would obey. Instead of working toward a New Jewish Free State, he inaugurated the presence of the Kingdom of God, in which *all* the people of God
will be reconciled under the one rule of God. This makes him our Saviour,
our Yeshuah.

The Christian faith relevant to Africa demands that we associate ourselves with the work of Christ in making the angels and dominations and powers his subjects (Col. 1:13–17), that is, subject to the Kingdom of God and its values. When we say we believe in Jesus or that Jesus saves, we are referring to the one through whom God demonstrated his sovereignty over all our experiences, including death. In the New Testament account of the events, God did not save Jesus from dying, but God rescued him from death after he had been declared dead, finished, his efforts come to nothing. The centurion who stood by reversed his views when he recognised the face of God in that death. Even more significantly, Jesus' death was transformed into a new quality of life, the style of which alone will reconcile us to God. It is a life lived perpetually in the presence of God. This resurrected life is in the hands of God alone.

The good news to Africa is that people and communities have to be willing to die to all that dehumanises on both personal and corporate levels. Those who believe that Christ lives forever, presenting us to God continually (Heb. 5:7; 7:25), will venture to live a life of total dependence on God by taking what he commands seriously. Jesus saves from the insecurity that breeds distrust in God. Herein lies the particularity of Christ, whatever the culture Christ relates to the needs of the people. Outside this practical context, our theological statements and formulations have little meaning.

In the pastoral letter written to Titus (3:5), we find a doctrine on which we are called to rely. In God's compassion he saves those who are misled and enslaved by passions and luxuries, those who live in wickedness and ill will, those who hate each other and are hateful themselves, by the water of rebirth and renewal in the Holy Spirit. People and communities in Africa, having experienced this rebirth, are then to be constantly reminded, as the early Christians were, of how God rescued the nation (Israel) from Egypt and afterwards destroyed those who did not trust him (Jude 5). All nations, all Christians, have to live in the knowledge of what Deuteronomy puts before Israel. A people saved by God have the Kingdom of God as their priority; this is the purpose for which Jesus lived and died. Liberated from the principalities and powers of this realm, we continue to work and live before God. That is salvation.

Footnotes

[1] If the Christian history of salvation includes a 'fall' that is the result of distrust and self-seeking, then the Christ-event becomes the only antidote. This raises, of course, the question of whether the myth quality of the fall degrades the story of salvation in the Christ-event.

[2] Literally, *yeshuah* is made up of the root word meaning 'to save', 'to give safety, ease' (*yeshua),* and the personal name for God, Yahweh. The English version of the name is Joshua and means 'Yahweh saves'. Since salvation is seen as coming only from God,

the word *yeshuah* has come to mean simply salvation, with no need to add 'of God'.

3 The word for deliver is *natsal*, 'to snatch or take away' – another common word associated with God-in-action.

4 In the context of the Akan world-view, atonement means reconciliation and is not concluded until the parties involved have joined in some act together such as sharing a meal. Such joint action is a pledge that the event that caused the discord will not be repeated. From this standpoint, picking any one theory of atonement does not satisfy the requirements for the rebuilding of community.

5 Baum, Gregory, *Religion and Alienation* (New York: Paulist Press, 1975), 37, discusses Karl Marx's insight into religion as being 'the sigh of the oppressed creature, the heart of a heartless world, and the soul of a soul-less condition'. Note that only after the foregoing did Marx pronounce the now popular dictum that 'religion is the opium of the people'. The Africanist version of this dictum is: 'They gave us the Bible and took our land', and accuses Christianity of being an alienating religion.

CHAPTER 4

Covenant and Community

Agreeing to live together

Covenants, testaments and agreements have always been aspects of our life in community. At every turn we figuratively put our signatures to various agreements, most of them documents we have not helped to draft but to which we have to give our assent if we are to operate normally in a given community. Your signature becomes the symbol of your acceptance of the terms of participation in a particular community.

Before westernisation, the Akan had several ways of ratifying covenants. When they pledged a piece of land, a rod was broken in two by the parties to the transaction and each kept half of it. (The Akan never sold land. The community of property arising from the community of blood made actual land sale difficult, if not impossible.) To ratify a marriage, an exchange of gifts took place between the two families. Purely social agreements were never made because they could not take place without libations, in which Onyame, Asaase Yaa and the ancestors were called upon to witness and to bless.

However, there were always agreements, primarily religious in nature. They were made to the divinities and are of the nature of Hannah's vow to Yahweh (I Sam. 1:9–18). I group vows of this kind with covenants because in primal religion, when divinities become inefficient or do not fulfil their part of the bargain, they simply lose devotees. In primal societies such as those encountered in parts of the Hebrew Scriptures, social agreements have a religious perspective as God is called upon to witness them. See, for instance, the treaty between Jacob and Laban (Gen. 31:49). The meaning of one of the three names given to the border between them is *Mizpah*, 'watch-post': 'Let Yahweh act as watch between us when we are no longer in sight of each other'. That God does watch is a firm belief among religious people. 'When you are busy making life miserable for others, God sees all parts of you, even those you try to hide, your innermost person is laid open to God.' So goes an Akan proverb.

Rather than focus on types of covenants, I would like to examine the cohesive role of covenants in the human community. Mulago of the Democratic Republic of Congo, formerly Zaïre, in a paper entitled 'Vital Participation, the Cohesive Principle of the Bantu Community', lists eight types of vital participation among the Bantu of Central Africa. The seventh type of participation is that of blood brothers. This union, he says, gathers into itself all the *baguma* or *bamwe* (Rwanda and Barundi words for the 'one', the unit, meaning all living or dead who descend from the same eponymous ancestor, all in whom the same life, the same blood, circulates in the paternal line – hence all members of the same family or clan). Blood brothers unite their two clans because the contracting parties drink one another's blood; they have, in effect, a shared communion in the same life.[1]

Because we Africans have our roots in the same soil, drink from the same river, or recognise the same divinity, a bond is created that one does not dream of breaking; it imposes a responsibility to each other that all endeavour to fulfil. Unity of life, therefore, is the cohesive principle in the African community. We human beings, with all created things, participate in life whose source is the One God. The enlightened world endorses Paul's quotation from the Stoics that God has made the earth and all the nations of the earth of one blood. This general principle is often forgotten and has to be recalled by specific covenants such as the blood-covenant practised between people of different clans, between members of the same cult, and sometimes even between a divinity and its devotees.[2] In most of these ceremonies, the blood is symbolised by a red liquid, just as wine represents the blood of Jesus Christ in the Christian Eucharist. The blood-covenant, as Mulago says,

> can never be added to a natural union, but imitates it, and has the purpose of extending it beyond the limits of the family and the clan. It thus transcends the racial and tribal setting and opens up vast possibilities for the expansion and widening of the family.[3]

The mixing of blood, a symbol of shared life, is binding, because between friends the blood-covenant actually involves mixing their lifeblood. The action underscores the sacredness and seriousness of all covenants.

Communion through shared meals takes place among people who are, or who wish to be, on peaceful and friendly terms. It is an extension of the everyday societal etiquette of the Akan, the Kikuyu and other African peoples, and is extended not only to members of one's family or friends but even to the casual caller or the stranger. To eat from the same dish is to enter into vital relationship with the other, hence, for me, the pathos and tragedy of the table talk in Mark's version of the Last Supper; 'It is one of the twelve, one who is dipping bread in the same dish with me' (Mk. 14:20). Shared meals conclude most social and ritual events; traditional festivals often conclude with the placing of food on graves to demonstrate our continued communion with those who have gone to the other world. This highlights the daily practice of putting bits of food and drops of water on the ground before eating and makes more meaningful the more elaborate calling on the ancestors through libation. To refuse to eat is a sign of hostility; hence the polite excuse of the Akan: 'My hand is in it'. We Africans come to the biblical covenants from a living experience of the seriousness with which our own covenants are made.

Old Testament covenants

The flood and the rainbow

After the great flood, God made a covenant with Noah (Gen. 8:20–22; 9:8–17) and with all living things. The rainbow was a sign, a visible and objective memorial of the promise of God. The Asante say that God is frowning when the dark rain clouds gather, and when the sun struggles through and a rainbow (Mfantse, *Nyankonton*) appears, children shout for joy. The 'Brow of God' arching clearly in the sky brings hope of a sunnier or at least a drier day.

Noah expresses his gratitude for God's past deeds by his sacrifice, but God's future, God's promise of sustained protection of creation, was entirely God's own initiative and entirely one-sided. God resolved out of compassion never again to visit the earth with such devastation. But the writer sets this unconditional protection in the context of directives on what to eat and on the injunction against homicide: 'I will surely require a reckoning ... of every man's brother I will require the life of man' (Gen. 9:5). This underscores the need to care for and protect others, the mutual respect for the other's being. Here the proper response to God's initiative is stipulated.

Abrahamic covenants

A second covenant is recorded by the priestly writers in Genesis 17. This time El Shaddai, the God of the mountains, says to Abraham: 'Walk before me, and be blameless. And I will make my covenant between me and you...' (Gen. 17:1–2). The terms of the covenant as laid down by El Shaddai include the promise to be the God not only of Abraham but of the generations that will descend from him. Here the writer places the origin of the obligation to circumcise the male, but more significant is the change in names of both the man and the woman. They were from henceforth to be known by names of God's choosing, names that were a transformation of their traditional ones. Naming is important in Africa; among the Yoruba, names that connect people with one or other of the four hundred divinities are transformed to bear more directly the presence of the Supreme God: *Fabunmi/Olubunmi* (Ifa gave me/God gave me), *Awokoya/Olukoya* (the secret cult rebuffs indignity/God rebuffs indignity).

In this covenant God dictated both sides of the obligation. Humanly speaking, the promises were ridiculous and 'Abraham fell on his face and laughed'

(Gen. 17:17), just as Sarah did later when God's messengers were to repeat the promise when she was within earshot (Gen. 18:12). Such promises could be made only by One who is totally in charge of the universe and of human history, but without the benefit of hindsight only the knowledge of God as entirely trustworthy makes them acceptable.

Covenant at Sinai

Exodus 19:5 tells us of a covenant made not with individuals but with a whole nation, the house of Jacob, the children of Israel. The whole nation was given a law to obey and fidelity to it was imposed. When they break it they invite the anger of God and forfeit the promises attached to obedience of the law.

Memory plays an important role here, as it did in Noah's covenant: when you see a rainbow you remember God's message by flood. It is the memory of a promise. Here the people were to call to mind events in which God acted to save them – 'remember what I did with the Egyptians' – as well as their own past experience of domination and exploitation – 'remember you yourselves were slaves'. The memory of their history was to keep them faithful to Yahweh and compassionate to the oppressed. If the God of all nations put an end to exploitation in one community, we cannot expect God to condone the same exploitation elsewhere and most especially not when it comes from a people who have themselves experienced exploitation and deliverance. The covenant becomes a memorial to God's determination to rid human nature of all domineering tendencies and to establish compassion in the human community.

The Sinai covenant also indicates that having agreed to be God's people, covenanting with other nations and powers is out of the question (Deut. 7:2). As a consecrated nation, a nation of priests, the Israelites recorded that God had directed them to an acceptable religion and that they were not to get mixed up with other religions. In a historical context, one appreciates how Israel, a small nation, had to ensure that its pastoral religion would not be overcome by the exuberant agricultural religions of its neighbours. The book of Deuteronomy shows a keen sense of this problem; it contains not only the core of the law but also several seemingly less important laws, regulating cooking, for example. All these ensured that the Israelites would be distinct from the Canaanites. The Ras Shamra tablets tell us that the Canaanites cooked their veal in milk: hence the Jewish injunction against cooking 'a kid in its mother's milk' (Ex. 23:19). Holding a common world-view is a prerequisite for perfect communion. The Hebrews operated on a strict principle of non-interaction with others for fear of losing their identity.

One element in the process of covenanting is the performance of sacrificial rites. This is of interest as it confirms our human experience of community-building as involving a readiness to sacrifice. Exodus 24:4 describes how Moses built an altar to God, made of twelve stones to symbolise the dedication of the twelve tribes of Israel to Yahweh. Then the people offered a holocaust to Yahweh as communion sacrifice, heard the law read, and gave their assent: 'We will be obedient' (Ex. 24:7). On the altar built for Yahweh, they threw half of the blood of the animals. 'And Moses took the blood and threw it upon the people, and said, "Behold the blood of the covenant which the Lord has made with you in accordance with all these words".' (v 8)

The final act as recorded in the Yahwist tradition (Ex. 24:1–2, 9–12) shows the elders going up and eating and drinking in the presence of God – God and human beings in one community, a community of interests to preserve true religion and true humanity. The blood of animals shared by the two parties sealed the agreement and symbolically united them. They now shared one life principle, a primal world-view that is also African. The ceremonies of the Day of Atonement (Lev. 23:26–32) have several parallels in the primal religions of Africa. These similarities enabled Africans to see in Christianity a clearer expression of what they had always known. But with human beings, knowing does not necessarily mean obeying.

The Israelites' failure to live up to the covenant is dramatically presented in the book of Judges (Judg. 2:16–19). Later Jeremiah gets to the heart of the matter: 'But let him who glories glory in this, that he understands and knows me, that I am the Lord who practices steadfast love, justice, and righteousness in the earth; for in these things I delight, says the Lord' (Jer. 9:24). The heart of the matter is that displaying external symbols of agreement (for example, wearing a wedding ring) does not guarantee one's faithfulness to the terms of the agreement. Therefore Yahweh will punish all those who are circumcised only in the flesh – Egypt, Judah, the sons of Ammon, Moab, the Arabs who live in the desert – all these nations and the whole house of Israel are uncircumcised at heart (Jer. 9:25). Jeremiah records God's promise that the new covenant will be in the heart of each person (31:31ff.). The individual's responsibility before God is never placed second; it runs concurrently with the communal pledge to obey God. Hence the need to highlight it, as seen in Ezekiel. But Ezekiel too, when he pictures renewal, sees the whole community wake up as a body, revitalised by the breath of God (Ezek. 36:26–27,37). Apart from this communal and individual axis, we also are responsible for one another's well-being (Ezek. 34:1–9,17–22).

New Testament covenant

This leads us naturally to the New Testament covenant formally proclaimed at the Last Supper by Jesus the Christ. We read in Mark's Gospel of 'my blood, the blood of the covenant' (14:24); in 1 Corinthians: 'Anyone who eats and drinks without discerning the body eats and drinks judgement upon himself' (11:29). Exasperated by the behaviour of the Christians at Corinth, Paul dramatises their lack of understanding of the covenant in his description, 'each one goes ahead with his own meal' (1 Cor. 11:21). Some go hungry, others get drunk. If you cannot have a communal meal, do not embarrass the poor. Respect their feelings; just eat in your own homes. Conspicuous consumption that ignores the needs of the poor, is a problem the church in Africa has to deal with, for not only are its individual members guilty of this evil, the church itself is often guilty. The church in Africa has often a very middle-class profile. Church architecture, vestments and interior decoration (including luxurious pipe organs) do not provide an atmosphere that is welcoming to the majority of African Christians. Yet all this is said to derive from the idea of worshipping in the beauty of holiness. Beauty has become the equivalent of a vulgar display of wealth; holiness is equated with that which is forbidding. The church becomes guilty of ostentation and conspicuous consumption, a style of life that alien-ates the majority of Africans who live under the burden of material poverty.

Paul sees the Christian covenant in the blood and body of Christ as uniting us with Christ (1 Cor. 10:14–22). The one bread, in which we all share, forms us into one body. Paul says: 'So we, though many, are one body in Christ, and individually members one of another' (Rom. 12:5).

The implications of this for divided Christianity are often discussed. Not only are we not in communion with other Christians, but we are divided into rich and poor, senders and receivers, black and white. We have even created two levels of being Christian with our lay and clergy structure. All this promotes divisiveness rather than diversity.

Covenant old and new

Africa faces a special problem at the centre of its covenant in Christ. 'You cannot drink the cup of the Lord and the cup of demons' (1 Cor. 10:21). On what basis do I decide between my mother's children and my brothers and sisters in Christ? When we assume that traditional covenants – because they are not made within the ambit of Christianity – are of the demon, we find our-selves in a dilemma.

Christian baptism presents us with an instance of this dilemma. Christian baptism, in that it washes away negative forces, is in perfect harmony with Africa's primal religious practices; the use of water to 'wash away' is present in several traditional yearly festivals and healing processes. The idiom used by the Fante to translate 'Christian baptism' comes from the ceremony that gives new life to one who has been sick – *Bo asu*. The opposite of *Bo asu* sounds almost the same: *Gu asu*, which implies actions calculated to mess up life for another person or for one's self. It was a toss up as to whether Christian baptism was to be *asubɔ* or whether the baptised were heading for self-destruction.

It did look like self-destruction since, in the early days, it was a sure sign that one had left one's traditional community, if not physically (which also happened), at least in mentality. Baptism as an incorporation into the Body of

Christ was a sacrament that could mean disloyalty to one's blood relatives. First, one was given a new name. This name often superseded the one given at the naming ceremony by one's grandparents – a name that had meaning for the family and was understood by the community. By that name a person was integrated into the community and began to be a social being. Giving that name up was social death.

The African Christian did literally receive a new name. Not only was it new, it was also strange, but pronounced to be 'best'. The person was marked for life as belonging to Christ. Excellent, if this mark did not also bring the 'stigma' of being a renegade from one's primal group. The new name Christians took with baptism meant opting out of being completely African, of belonging to a particular ethnic group; indeed, it meant opting out of the human family. Your mother and father become those who do the will of God and seek God's Kingdom.

Some African Christians have sought to reconcile the two naming ceremonies by asking a Christian priest to baptise the child in the context of the traditional naming ceremony. But are the two covenants coterminous? The ethnic ceremony excludes 'outsiders' as being 'strangers', but not necessarily enemies or inferiors. With the belief that all human beings are the children of God, *Nnipa nyinaa yε Onyame mma*, cross-group alliances are made to the benefit of all concerned. Their common interest binds them into a new community and thus widens their world. Superimposing Christian baptism on the traditional naming ceremony would be like making a blood covenant involving an individual member of the family without requiring that person to cease to have the well-being of the natural family at heart. Africans accepted Christian names as additional names and used them in church, at school, and for civil obligations of colonial structures. At home and for personal rites, the name given at the traditional naming ceremony was used.[4]

African Christians became incorporated into the church and into Christ without giving up their incorporation into their human family. The situation has parallels in the early church. Christianity was launched as a universal religion based only on the acceptance of the Lordship of Christ Jesus. Its struggle was to be accepted without antagonising the civil powers, but it clearly set out to demonstrate that its world-view superseded those of the ethnic religions with which it competed. The universal triumphed over the particular, but not without being expanded, modified and redefined. Theologising our baptism as African Christians means examining the implications of our two names, African and Christian, and the two covenants involved in the ceremonies that incorporate us into two communities. The core of relationships – person to person and community to community – is examined as we examine our covenants.

What do these covenants, Christian and otherwise, aim at achieving? I believe they serve to line us up, for God and humanity and against all that is of the demon. We live in a world full of demons and idols more sophisticated than any that our primal society ever knew, and we need to name them so that we may confront them. These idols have proved to be anti-life and have taken over our world. Our covenants with the demon are called a 'balance of power' and they threaten to override our communion in Christ. It is the same with the idol called state security and the devil's own symbol, material wealth.

Living according to our Christian covenant demands that we say with the writer of Ephesians: 'Putting away falsehood, let every one speak the truth with his neighbour, for we are members one of another' (4:25). Let us live our lives before the One God whose will is that the human community should conform to the values of the Kingdom of God. When we are able to do this, then we can begin to appreciate the implications of baptism and the Eucharist as sacraments building up not only our community with one another as human beings, but also with God in whose image we are made and whose name is engraved on our hearts.

From the perspective of Africa, an interpretation of the Eucharist that highlights the aspect of sacrifice is one that will touch people's spirituality in such a way as to affect their lives. The victory that comes out of sharing what really costs us something, is for Africans a living experience. This is our path to triumph over exploitation and domination, and the way to replace charity with justice.

The link between our baptism and our frequent participation in the Eucharist is well made when we are reminded to be ready to share the baptism with which Mark begins the story of the work of Jesus, as well as the bitter cup of the crucifixion, which Jesus referred to as his baptism. The Eucharist becomes a communion, a covenant uniting us to share his mission of proclaiming and demonstrating what life under God looks like. If we wish to share the Kingdom of God then we have to be ready to accept the costly sacrifice implied in our baptism. Our sacrificial life was implied by our membership in the African community and, with the coming of Christ, it has been clearly demonstrated as attainable.

Footnotes

[1] Mulago Gwa Cikala Musharhamina, 'Vital Participation: the Cohesive Principle of the Bantu Community', in Dickson, Kwesi A., and Paul Ellingworth (eds.), *Biblical Revelation and African Beliefs* (London: Lutterworth Press, 1969), 141–42.

[2] Mulago, 'Vital Participation', 154.

[3] Mulago, 'Vital Participation', 155.

[4] Among the Akan, the name a person is given depends on the day on which that person is born. The name given is known as the *kradin*, 'soul-name'. On the eighth day after birth at least one other name is added. One carries these names throughout life. Marriage does not change them. These are the names ingrained on the personality and the only ones deemed spiritually efficacious.

II. Global Issues in African Perspective

CHAPTER 5

Conversations on Peace
(A letter to Milan Opocensky on his 65th birthday)

They have treated the hurt of my daughter in an off-handed manner.
They have cried harmony when the reality is suppression and apathy.
They know no more the meaning of peace, for injustice is their daily
bread. (Echoes of Jer. 8:11; Is. 59:8)

In West Africa where we have Muslims, and where the Yoruba language is
heard everywhere, two words that we all come to know are *alafia* and
salaam. They are words of greeting, and we love to greet. In greetings we
take the time to ask of the welfare of all, people and business alike. The
common greeting among Muslims is *salaam*. It is an enquiry after welfare
and about peace. The Yoruba response, *alafia*, says it is health and peace
that accompany us today. All greetings enquire about health in a comprehensive way. Responses include 'It is well, by the grace of God', 'We are
managing', 'The world is hard', 'The going is tough'. 'Our ears are never
cool' is the literal translation of 'We have no peace'. 'Our chests are not
cool': it is full of anger and dissatisfaction borne out of deceit and exploitation. Young Americans say 'cool' in appreciation. I wonder what young
Africans will say 'cool' to. There seems to be very little in Africa one can
say 'cool' to. There is no *alafia* and no *salaam* except in our greetings.
Some who are not Africans will even tell us that hope in Africa is dead and
that Africa has been forgotten by the rest of the world. That, of course, is a
lie.

Peace in conversations about Africa refers to the absence of war in the
first (and often only) instance. It would seem that war has been the style of
life for many human communities in many generations. Today we can see
Rwanda and Bosnia and Ireland live, and are shocked. For long periods
there were no TV cameras to record the atrocities and to relay the inhu-
manities of war instantly to the rest of the world. Imagine if we were all
privy to what went on in the Americas, Australia, or southern Africa when
Europeans expropriated land from indigenous peoples and massacred them.
Imagine if we all saw live what we see reconstructed in *Schindler's List*?
The world has been built on war and our '*pax* this' and '*pax* that' have been
won with bullets and the threat of bullets.

Our Common Heritage

Among Christians, and especially theologians, conversations on peace have sparked off intense reflections. Often we conclude, 'If only we knew where our peace lies!' What marks our discussions is the acknowledgement and the insistence that we have not plumbed the depth of the meaning of peace when we have described it as the antithesis of war. In ecumenical circles, and especially in the World Student Christian Fellowship (WSCF) of the 1960s and 1970s, these discussions were linked with the existential situations around the world where people struggled to preserve their humanity and where many young people were seeking alternatives to the unjust structures they had come to despise. What marks the WSCF – the context in which I first met Milan – is its attention to the holistic development of young people. Its theological explorations have always touched the contemporary political and economic structures within which people must operate. The now two decades old Ecumenical Association of Third World Theologians (EATWOT) is also marked by the attention to the situation in which Christians struggle to live as the body of Christ and to present the gospel. Contextual theology has taught us that to be faithful to the gospel, we have to take the daily life experiences of people and communities seriously. Jesus did just that.

This essay is a tribute to one who was among many voices in the WSCF in the 1960s calling attention to the need to rethink socialism in the context of Christianity. The growing signs of the failure of the system to provide a sense of worth of the individual beyond being an economic being, and the failure of the capitalist ideology to take cognisance of the marginalisation of the majority of the people who live under its aegis, were a central concern of young ecumenists, and leadership was provided by the WSCF. This approach to theology is part of what in Europe was designated as 'political theology'. It was ignored by some, while feared and marginalised by others for being dangerous. But times have changed. Even in the European theological world, several eminent theologians are lending their weight to the integrity of the theological approach that sees peace, justice and ecological harmony as strands of a single web and recognises that theology needs to take people's location into consideration if it is to be good news. Theologians in EATWOT have been struggling with a similar hermeneutics in their task of articulating the emerging theologies of their regions. With the Cold War going against communism, many were sure that a liberation theology that drew on Marxist analysis would have no more standing. But dismantling the Berlin wall has not ended the exploitation of the poor, nor has it ended the gross economic inequalities that are our common experience world-wide.

In these theological efforts, the word *justice* has been the key in opening up for analysis the malaise of the human condition. The absence of peace, personal, communal and global, was traced to the lack of right relationships. The swarming of Europeans into Aotearoa/New Zealand, Australia and (most tellingly) South Africa, could not be celebrated by Africans and other peoples of the 'First Nations' of these regions. The spilling over of Europe into the Americas some 500 years ago did not spell peace or justice for the indigenous people there. It was in 1992 a real eye-opener for some of us that the European descendants of 'Latin America' could think of the word 'celebrate' to mark this event and rejoice to name the whole region 'Latin', when it is the home of people some of whom are not of Latin descent and do not claim Latin as the root of their language. The arrogance of Europe and people of European descent knows no bounds! In Africa we began to protest the injustice of the European stance in their new-found unity and solidarity over against all other peoples. We asked, 'What kind of Europe will 1992 bring?' As if we could not have guessed. We asked, 'How will this new Europe affect the rest of the world?' As if there were any doubt about the European view of the rest of the world that is not of European descent.

Conversations on peace

In 1989, John Ferguson, a friend of the Student Christian Movement (SCM) of Nigeria, asked me for reflections on peace. John was a pacifist and a theologian; Milan was associated with the Christian Peace Conference and is a theologian, indeed was teaching theology in Prague, his home. John has passed on, and Milan has turned 65, but the legacy of peace which they and others of the WSCF have nourished, deserves to be nurtured as our language has become 'peace with justice'. Hence my return to that subject in this tribute to Milan.

What I did was to talk with a number of theologians from the Third World that I met at various conferences and gatherings. All the conversations were held during December 1989, the season of goodwill in which we mark the presence of the 'Prince of Peace' among us. As I read over them seven years later, they still ring true and relevant.

Peace and liberation

Theologians of the Third World and others from minority cultures around the world, recognising that the roots of the lack of *shalom* in their world include the inability to say one's own word about God, have been making vigorous attempts in the past three decades to discover the spirituality of the peoples among whom they live. Their commitment is to stand in solidarity with the poor. They are part of the community of the poor who cry to God for justice, and who know no peace except the peace that comes from resignation.

Third World theologians, especially those from Latin America, began a 'prophetic theology', moved by 'passion and compassion' and based on their involvement in the liberation struggles in the places where they lived. Liberation theology speaks of the *shalom* that issues forth from justice and results in people proclaiming with contentment, 'We feel cool'. Health, wholeness, a sense of well-being, the absence of debt and the existence of good relations between persons and peoples: liberation theologians say that all this is within the reach of the whole of humanity if we can attain justice.

But what do liberation theologians say now, when the revolutions in Latin America have all quietened down into seeking the involvement of the civil society in the redefinition of power? People ask, 'Now that socialism is in shambles, how can these theologians hold on to Marxist hermeneutics?'

Raising peace as an issue in 1989, I sensed a kind of impatience with the word. For me this was understandable as most of the people came from situations where there was not even 'the absence of war'. To talk about peace was not a luxury they allowed themselves; their energy had to go into seeking peace. The silences in the conversations were as eloquent as the statements. It was as if these friends and colleagues were asking: 'What have we been writing about all this time, if it is not about peace? Peace is not a subject for theses and theories, it is an experience to be struggled for. It is as part of this struggle and prayer for peace that we do liberation theology.' Peace is leaving the children of Nicaragua to grow up in an atmosphere of justice and respect for human life. 'Peace,' said a Korean woman, 'calls for consideration for Korean families separated by two world powers who are peddling competing ideologies and whose interest is more in political and economic hegemony than in the daily hurts and well-being of flesh and blood human beings.' Today there is no Cold War but Korean people are still divided.

Talking of peace

What these friends were saying to me was: 'Those who seek peace have to resist dehumanisation'. To talk about peace in the Third World is to highlight the situation of exploitation in the South that has been the result of Western Europe's colonial expansion. It is to talk about stolen land, stolen dignity, stolen humanity. It is to talk about imposed religions and enforced cultural hegemony. It is to talk of exploited labour and of racism. To talk about peace in the Third World is to point to situations of neo-slavery that make nations replace food crops with cash crops, receive a pittance for their labours, use that pittance to pay 'debts' owed to their trading partners, and then face hunger at home as if they never made an effort. It is to expose the reality of trade relations which make it necessary for the rich to lend to the poor, so that the poor can pay interest to the rich, to enable the rich to become more affluent. It is to expose the new name of colonialism known as globalisation. To talk about peace in Africa is to point to the feminisation of poverty and the multiple oppression of the African woman. It is to expose situations in which young women have to show evidence of birth control measures when they seek employment. To talk about peace in Africa is to get at the roots of the exodus of young people from rural areas into cities, and of the able-bodied of Africa into the lands of those who have exploited the continent for generations.

With significant exceptions, most of the contemporary armed conflicts in the world are raging in the South. Almost without exception, the weapons are supplied by the North. The economic dependence of the North on the arms industry is too well attested to need any discussion here. One is not being cynical to suspect that the North fuels conflicts and wars to keep that industry flourishing. The racial, cultural and religious pluralism of the South has a tendency to spark off conflict, especially when the economic atmosphere is also unhealthy. It is clear, however, that but for the participation of the North by way of arms deals, these frays could not reach the proportions we have known.

Bernadeen Silva, in an article, 'Sinhala/Tamil Conflict: An Obstacle to the Building of a Democratic Socialist System in Sri-Lanka', focuses on the 'agonising problem (that) keeps erupting in acts of violence of degrading forms'. Silva x-rays a situation in which race and religion breed disharmony. Herself a Sri-Lankan, she saw her nation's situation in the wider context of 'racism in South Africa, racial discrimination as experienced in Britain, the USA, Australia and in some countries in Latin America and Asia'. She saw the cause of violence in the Third World within the wider context of nation-building, the creation of modern economies and the role of multinationals.

Back in 1975, Silva suggested to the International Commission of the Christian Peace Conference that violence is inevitable if 'problems of poverty and misery prevail, but that there can be a lasting strategy of co-operation between all who believe in peace, love and justice ... necessary for the creation of the new person'. She went on to say that 'to seek peace is to become an integral part of the project that has as its goal the creation of a new society (a new Jerusalem), a new style of life, that launches an offensive against disparities in wealth, power and responsibility'. Fear and the machine gun will not bring a new society; only a qualitative change of heart towards justice and love will give us peace.

From South Africa, where reconciliation and patience were preached by the church to the Black Africans for years, came a reappraisal of what reconciliation requires. In the epoch-making *Kairos Document* and in the writings of South African theologians, the word 'reconciliation' was firmly located in the context of liberation from injustice and oppression. 'Reconciliation,' said Allan Boesak, 'requires love.' In the context of laws that serve the economic and political interests of the rich and powerful, there can be no reconciliation without confrontation, no forgiveness without prior repentance and confession of sin. The speech of Namibia's Sally Mondlane at a meeting of the American Association of University Women in October 1986 summed up the South African situation at that time of intense debates on sanctions as follows: 'Without sanctions we suffer without hope, with sanctions we suffer in hope'.

Talking with the late Sally Mondlane was for me itself an experience of the power of hope in the struggle for peace and justice. Teresa Okure, a Nigerian theologian with whom I shared this experience later, said, while reflecting on Rom. 8:18–25, 'No woman goes into labour when there is no hope of a child being born'. What was happening in South Africa at the time was described by her as the birth pangs of a new society, within whose boundaries will be found the fruits of justice and love for the neighbour which are some of the signs of peace.

Sharing my anguish over how we have managed to disturb the peace that Christmas celebrates, Gloria Chun from Taiwan said to me, 'When people in power put harmony before peace, they stand ready to kill for their ideas, but not to work for the *shalom* of all'. Ideologies that capture people's being and lead them to believe that ideas are more precious than people, become idols, and where an idol reigns there is no room for God and therefore no room for that *shalom*, that wholeness of life that occurs and recurs in contemporary African theology as a prayer and a hope.

A concrete and holistic approach

The war in the Gulf states (1991) sparked off a debate at the seventh Assembly of the World Council of Churches that reminded one of the 'just war' discussions of yesteryear. Discussions of peace in times of armed conflict by people well away from the scenes of conflict, tend to jump straight to war and pacifism, violence and non-violence. These ideological debates almost always cloud the life and death issues that the antagonists face daily. My reading of the Third World and conversations with its theologians and Christians lead me to say that a major shift has to be made by peace movements in their approach to peace. Maybe they are in the best position to do something about the 'limited wars', labelled 'low intensity conflicts', that are promoted and fought mainly in the Third World, and are a major contributor to its material poverty. The peace factor that I see in the writings of the Third World theologians is centred around the motif of the reign of God over a humanity made in the image of God. These people cover the face of the earth and their peace is linked up as one in God's world. Women, pursuing liberation through a struggle to dismantle patriarchy, have not only pointed to the injustice and the violence perpetrated against women, but have also joined environmentalists to pursue a holistic approach to peace. Peace is not only a matter in the human community, it also has to do with our relationship to the world.

Since the WCC Assembly of 1983 in Vancouver, the Council has tried to promote this holistic, approach of justice, peace and ecological harmony. At the seventh Assembly held in Canberra, it became clear that pursuing this demands more maturity than we had so far exhibited. Ecological issues are bringing before us the need for a deeper theology of creation. When we call for a dialogue, a review or a renewal, we cannot but ask, 'Who controls the current world-view?' The theologies and ideologies that rule the contemporary world have their proponents and their beneficiaries who naturally begin to feel threatened.

Pursuing peace

Why am I saying all this to Milan? These conversations took place seven years ago. Since then, we have seen the fall of the Berlin wall replaced by the horrors of Bosnia and the threat of another divided city in the making. We have seen stronger barriers raised in Europe against Africans and some Asians who dream of attaining *shalom* in Europe. We have seen the walls of apartheid crumble and the struggle for *shalom* for all begin in South Africa, but we have yet to see the beginning of *shalom* in Sudan, Rwanda, Liberia, do I dare leave out any African country? So from conversations on peace offered to John Ferguson, a friend of the SCM of Nigeria and a theologian, I turn to Milan, a theologian who has taught Nigerians in his home city, Prague, with a challenge to seek joint action for *shalom*.

Sixty-five years ago Milan was a baby fed on milk and tears. For years he has wept the tears of God. He belongs to the people I know who have absorbed the tears of the world and agonised over the lack of *shalom* for the majority of God's people. On his birthday I sent him a greeting, part of which said:

> While the struggle continues, we share this agony together ... I am calling attention to peace now because (I sense that) the affluent world is going to relate to you and yours more or less as they have done with Africa. People of the Third World and now those of the Central and Eastern parts of the newly united Europe live in a complex and precarious situation that is a challenge to all who would seek peace and pursue it.

The gospel tells us that if we seek to save our life, we shall lose it. This saying was not addressed to people whose lives were in physical danger, or whose humanity was being eroded and degraded, but to people fumbling towards the true meaning of human existence. It is a word in season to all of us. Peace and violence are a challenge to all world religions, not just to Christianity. Paths to peace are rugged and demand tougher strategies than verbal denunciations of violence that do not provide alternatives beyond turning the other cheek.

The need to convert nations to non-violent solutions to conflicting demands is endorsed by all, even while they continue to seek solutions by violence. It is generally agreed that action for peace is no longer a luxury and cannot be reduced to academic debate. Nor can it be left in the hands of the few who demonstrate regularly for peace and for the 'greenness' of the earth, still less in the hands of the few who sit at negotiation tables, for even while they talk, the acts of violence and of exploitation thrive unimpeded. Peace with justice demands the concerted efforts and action of all human beings.

Christian communities have long displayed this concern. With the worsening of human and international relations, ministries of peace education have been put in place. Ethical exhortation alone will not meet the need of the world. To have an impact, Christian efforts must become more comprehensive and deal seriously with political, economic and cultural realities. Nothing can be achieved without dialogue with people of other faith communities who are also struggling to walk the path of peace.

People like Milan are in a position to bridge the gulf between African theologians and the theologians of Central and Eastern Europe. We need this contact lest 'attention to Eastern Europe means the death of Africa'. A globalisation of what it means to live the *shalom* intended by God is demanded by the globalisation of the power of those who would rule the world by economic success. It has been too long a letter, but the agenda of peace with justice is also not short.

CHAPTER 6

The People Next Door

(An essay in honour of Kosuke Koyama)

'And who is my neighbour?' was the question posed to Jesus by one who had fulfilled the requirements of the law. What more does one have to do to express the fullness of life we are expected to live before God? The reflections offered in this essay are based on a view of life which affirms that the concentric circles of relationships experienced by all human beings require a sensitivity to the presence of the other and to the centre which is Ultimate Being, God. Life in community is, for me, a spiritual matter, hence the centring on God. Secondly, community is a web that links all together and, as such, underlines the interdependence and mutual accountability of neighbours.

This study of neighbourliness will call attention to three strands in this complex web of life and conclude with a suggestion of what it means to love the neighbour as one's self. In all the discussion, I shall draw upon my experience of Africa, the neighbourhood I know best, although for many years I had substantial residence in Europe and North America and interacted with persons of varying geographical locations as friends, colleagues and worshippers.

Who is my neighbour?

The marks of neighbourliness were defined by Jesus in the parable of the Good Samaritan whom I name the Compassionate Other. The parable sets a scene of the evil of violent exploitation of an other, and the sanctimonious notions of purity and pollution that result in an inadequate understanding of what religion demands. We are presented with good people who were so intent on fulfilling their religious duties that they could not stop to recognise the work of evil or counter it with life-giving moves. They were tuned into a type of righteousness that would be soiled by getting mixed up with 'ritual pollution'. Acting as neighbour called for a different type of righteousness. With Jesus' understanding of life, one can raise the question: How can you say you worship, love and hold God worthy, when you despise, ignore, or leave God's handiwork to perish?

Neighbourliness, for Jesus, consists in stopping by the scene of disaster, caring for what faces perdition, using one's resources and one's time to restore life where death threatens to take over. It is going out of one's way to seek the well-being of the other. The parable of Luke 10:29–37 is replayed in Matthew 25:31–46, the parable of the Last Judgement, set in an eschatological dimension. The thirsty, the hungry, the homeless and the captive are neighbours, persons calling on our resources of compassion, people whose sufferings are ours by virtue of their humanity and the humanity of Jesus of Nazareth.

The neighbour is not only the person who is geographically 'next door' but whoever and whatever is threatened with annihilation and a return to chaos. The planet earth exists in a 'heavenly' neighbourhood, the world is a neighbourhood of the created, among whom are human beings with their classification into races, classes and communities of faith. Human existence takes place within concentric circles of relatedness: family, nurture, culture, nationality and racial identification make us into particular human beings. The question of who is my neighbour signifies the fact that often we live oblivious of the existence of the other, yet the unacknowledged neighbour is still a neighbour.

The earth, a neighbourhood

The earth is our home. We have no other, and our survival depends on its health and wholeness. Studies of environment have called our attention to the larger neighbourhood within which our human communities develop. Planet earth belongs in a heavenly environment that it responds to and to which we, in turn, relate. As earth dwellers, our lives are in constant relationship with the sun, the moon and the atmosphere around us. On earth, other beings are our neighbours – plants, animals – some too small for eyes to behold and others much larger than we are. Mountains and rivers are so imposing that we sometimes feel them as the habitation of being that is different and more potent than we are. Minerals, solid, liquid and gaseous, are all our neighbours. Contemporary ecological sensitivities have underlined the principles of connectedness, interdependence and mutual sustainability. When air and water and vegetation are in danger, human life too is endangered. With the awareness of ecology, human vision of neighbourliness has begun to expand to include all creation, seen and unseen. Loving our neighbour has come to mean recycling, reforestation and cleaning up the waters around us. It is interesting that the African biologist, Wangari Maathai, sees 'the environmental movement as part and parcel of the pro-democracy movement'. Wanton exploitation of the other goes with the marginalisation of the other through decision-making. It imposes silence on all and takes away the voices of humans while it refuses to hear the groanings of the rest of creation.

The world of human beings, land masses, regions and nations, is linked together by human conquest of space. This geographical world has become a neighbourhood bound together by political links and communication technology. The human species, now divided into races, does not live in geographi-

cally separate spaces. Few human communities can claim uniformity of physical features. Having created a United Nations, all races find themselves in the
position of neighbours and face the challenge of working out their interactions
and relationships across round-tables. The classification of humans on the basis
of socio-economic status, which remains with us, does not nullify the fact that
we are in constant interaction, even when we prefer to operate as cliques. Even
grouping human beings into faith communities no longer circumscribes neighbourhood, though we may prefer not to have to recognise the validity and
power of other religions. The earth is, willy-nilly, our common neighbourhood.

In the three circles of neighbourhoods – planetary, geographical and human
– the last two challenge us to review our understanding of neighbourliness.
Our environment is full of unacknowledged neighbours, all who are in need of
survival, healing, or affirmation and call for our understanding and practice
of neighbourliness. We know who our neighbour is. The challenge is how to
live as neighbours in the family and culture that have made us and how to
derive and cultivate resources for nurturing global neighbourliness from these
primary experiences. Christians believe that God was agitated enough about
this to come and physically join our earthly neighbourhood.

A community of neighbours

Associating with Europeans and Americans, I have come up very often
against the hurdle of what family is. Is your family with you? Or, even more
strange to my ears, do you have a family? Whatever meaning we assign to
the word *family*, its value to human development is undoubtedly high. What
we are today depends to a large extent on whom we had for family when we
were growing up. There is an adage in Akan that is popularly translated as
'Alone is miserable'. *Baako yɛ yaw* captures the African rejection of indi-
vidualism and aloneness. To lose one's place in, or lose touch with, one's
family is the worst possible misfortune. World-wide, the smallest human
community that makes us social beings with power to communicate and gifts
and skills to contribute, is the family. We developed relationships and learned
who was who in that smallest of communities. From there we were launched
toward our nearest neighbours, the people next door. We were nurtured and
socialised and acculturated. We became conscious of difference and nationality. We learned citizenship and nationalism. We learned what is expected of
us in the various sub-groups that make up our world.

For Africans, religion and ethics are high on the agenda of socialisation. A
respected member of the Akan community to which I belong, is a good
person who thinks and lives by what is good. A person with *adwenpa*, a good
mind or brain, is not simply an intelligent person but a good person, humble,
generous and brave, a community-minded person. Unless one has these qualities, an Akan community will not make one a leader.[1] However, if a person

has all these but has any physical disability or injury, he or she cannot become a king or queen. Royalty is symbolic of excellence and security. Royal leaders, more than everybody else in the community, should exhibit the benedictions for which the Akan pray: God's grace, peace, good visual and auditory powers, fertility, and prosperity.[2] These high ideals create their own marginalisation, for the community is extremely adamant about its definition of fullness and wholeness. Families will spend their all to enable one to regain one's health of mind and body or overcome impotence and infertility, but would not think of the possibility of changing traditional attitudes toward such 'handicaps'. These handicaps are considered disgraceful, and *animguase mfata okaniba* ('to be dead is better than to be alive and disgraced'). Applying the principle to fertility, Okyeame Amoateng of Kumasi concludes that to be impotent or sterile is worse than death.[3] Therefore neighbourliness requires that one is helped to overcome these symbols of death, but there the compassion ends. No transformation is envisaged, and so in this most caring community, one finds unneighbourliness arising from the fear of ritual impurity.

The ethics that govern relationships and neighbourliness among the Akan are expressed in symbols, proverbs and maxims. The traditional symbols are printed on Akunintam cloth (the cloth of the great warriors) and on Adinkra cloth (the parting cloth traditionally meant for funerals and memorials). The symbols of the latter have been greatly popularised, hence their use here to highlight what an Akan community expects of its members and those with whom it deals. The most central idea of community is that of unity in diversity. This is represented by two crocodiles who share one stomach (Siamese twins). The symbol points out that it is unnecessary for people whose destinies are joined together to struggle for a larger share of the available resources. Community of property and mutual aid used to be a cardinal principle among the Akan. As a people, the Akan abhor covetousness, greed and all egocentrism, and believe that affluence and power are the result of togetherness.

'One's neighbour's day is one's day'; one's trouble is bound to affect one's neighbour. Many proverbs, sayings, and folktales underline this principle. The Adinkra symbol of four hearts joined together teaches togetherness and unity in thought and deed. There is a recognition that disharmony is possible in a community, but the symbol and proverb relating to tongue and teeth say that although they quarrel occasionally, that is never a reason for parting company. The community warns its members not to bite one another and presents them with the qualities of fair play, peace, forgiveness, unity and harmony. The need for co-operation in situations of interdependence is represented by a chain which also marks the unity that is the strength of a community.

The solidarity and security one expects to find in a community is captured in the symbol of the enclosed compound, the traditional quadrangle housing several generations that belong to a lineage, as well as some who are related as clients and spouses. This safety and care is also symbolised by a fence. Within the fence are one's closest neighbours; outside the fence, diplomacy and caution are needed. Within the fence, one is expected to be truthful, strong, brave, ingenious, creative, loving, wise, patient, just, intelligent, generous, alert, obedient, and so on, but all these qualities are to be available for the maintenance of the health, security, and welfare of the community.

The community disapproves of all that brings death or negates the above qualities. Sins and taboos are made known so that offenders have themselves to blame for the punishment they get, for what they do or fail to do brings negative influences that affect the whole community and has to be expiated with rituals and sacrifices.[4] The Akan abhor murder, suicide, stealing, insincerity and hypocrisy. They frown upon pride and ostentatiousness. Ingratitude, selfishness, laziness, filthy habits, lasciviousness and sorcery are all things that break or undermine community and therefore are to be avoided. A healthy neighbourhood will vigilantly monitor interpersonal relationships to ensure good neighbourliness.

These community norms, mores and ethics are rooted in a common culture that includes the belief in a Supreme Being, Onyame, who sanctions all the ethical requirements. People believe that they live under the keen eyes of their ancestors, who are concerned that traditions that have enabled the community to survive, are diligently kept. In other words, neighbourliness is guided by religion and culture. The concept raises critical questions for intercommunal relations. Here one could say that our parable does not help us, for we do not know the ethnic origin of the person who lay brutalised. On the other hand, Jesus could be interpreted as saying the ethnic origin of the neighbour is immaterial. Of no consequence also is the ethnic origin of the robber or robbers, the exploiters and other agents of death. The critical root here is their common origin in the one God.

Continuing with the Akan as model community within the national neighbourhood of Ghana, we can ask: Do the Akan see and behave toward their neighbours to the north, the Hausa, as children of the one God? Do Ghanaians extend neighbourliness to other Africans? Do Africans extend neighbourliness to Europeans? In all cases, one should ask, Is this neighbourliness reciprocated? From the geographical/spatial model, one could ask other types of questions. Is there reciprocal neighbourliness between Hindus and Moslems, across racial fences, between homosexuals and heterosexuals, rich and poor, young and old? How do we respond to variety and difference? Does neighbourliness stop at the fence? This brings us to our second locus of hospitality, the world.

We began by assuming that the particular label of the one in need is of no consequence. But let us suppose the wounded man was a Jew. A Jew, taught to have no dealings with a Samaritan, allowed himself to receive the neighbourly act of 'the filthy other'. The people we despise, those of 'lower rank', those with unmentionable diseases, those we label as causing social problems – they too can be neighbourly. But can we bring ourselves to let *them* touch *us*? Jesus, the paradigm shifter, asked for water from a Samaritan woman. Those we have been taught to avoid because they are less than we are, have it in them to be neighbourly. They too are made in God's image. They have a womb that becomes agitated at the sight of suffering and injustice. When the Samaritan saw the wounded Jew, he had compassion on him. Like God, his womb turned and so he did what God does to people who have been cast aside to die. Those our religion and culture teach us to ostracise, God draws back into the orbit of compassion and neighbourliness, whether they are wounded Jews or marginalised Samaritans. The neighbourly act is a Godlike act. Imagine, the wounded Jew woke up to discover that his survival had been assured by the compassion of a Samaritan. Does he feel polluted by this touch and try to forget it?

The world as a neighbourhood

Jet travel, communication and the information explosion have joined the traditional trade routes and patterns of migration to make the world into one neighbourhood. Here we would like to discuss race, class and faith communities as the loci of variety that could either threaten or enrich the practice of neighbourliness. The African communal ideology illustrated above does not produce a closed community. It is a flexible entity that expands to include those who prove themselves hospitable and understand life as a continuum, and human relations and humanity as in process of evolving and becoming. We have all been children, but none has a prior experience of adulthood. We are all learning together.

Nobody has seen it all before, so there is always room for new ideas, as well as for benefiting from the experience of others. For this reason, membership in the community is not closed. There is always room for one more person, as long as the person is ready to participate in creating the community and has not come with inflexible dogmas. Welcoming difference, diversity and variety, demands a sensitivity to the needs of the whole community as well as respect for every member, irrespective of the difference that marks them. There is no one who has nothing to contribute to the community, hence hospitality is expected from all and due to all.

One identification mark that distinguishes persons in the global community is what we have come to label 'race'. Humans, as a biological species, have been subdivided into races on the basis of physical characteristics. Colour, broadly described as black or white, has been a fundamental issue in human relations since Europeans overran Africa, the Americas, Australia, Aotearoa/New Zealand and other islands in the Pacific Ocean and the Caribbean, in search of land, wealth, and fame. Africa, the nearest neighbour to Western Europe (the home of early European adventurers), took the brunt of the absence of neighbourliness that governed the minds of these early Europeans. To be able to perform the atrocities that gave them land and wealth, they convinced themselves that the 'dark races' were not human and therefore could be exploited and disposed of with impunity, in the same fashion as the rest of earth's resources, which they claimed God had put at the disposal of the white race of Europe. It was inconceivable that black people and white people, dark people and pale people, could live together as neighbours. Racism is the antithesis of neighbourliness. When one is not of your race, you owe them nothing but contempt.

The satiated neighbour

Where race was not the barrier to neighbourliness, social location took over, especially as class based on the economic status of persons. In many human settlements, 'birds of the same feather flock together', the rich on one side, the poor on the other. In-between, grades of wealth and poverty divided people. The African communal ideology succeeded in curbing the tendency for social location – royalty, access to land, education and training – to develop toward a rigid class system identified by wealth. The principle of hospitality undermines it. The Akan say, 'It is one person who hunts down the elephant to provide meat for the whole village'. Abundance is for sharing. With this view of hospitality, Europeans were made at home in Africa, and Africans were surprised that the Europeans turned out to be predators. They turned out to be people whose eyes are shut to the humanity of the other. 'If you hate me, close your eyes.' The Akan believe that you cannot do evil to one whose eyes you can see. It seems, however, that the coming of class with westernisation has meant that people can close their eyes and not see the humanity of the people they wrong. One who is not of your class ceases to be in your neighbourhood.

In the global neighbourhood, class and race seem to coincide at many points. In Africa, apartheid crystallised this for us. The phenomenon operates globally. Most of the countries whose people have to swallow the humiliating pill of structural adjustment programmes (SAP) imposed by moneylenders, are also predominantly black. The moneylenders are predominantly white, European, or of European descent who got an economic lift on the backs of the peoples they colonised or whose lands they appropriated. The terms, black and white, North and South, are being used here to mark the economic equator that divides the world and is also found in every state. The South is poor, and its inhabitants are black and exploited. The North is rich, and its inhabitants are white and comfortable. The nuances to this caricature are many, for on the one hand, there exist in wealthy countries people who are structurally marginalised and cannot dip into the wealth that is available. On the other hand, there are a few in the poor countries who are, by the standards of the North or in comparison with their immediate neighbours, wealthy because they participate directly in the wealth of the North or off the crumbs that fall from the master's table. In Africa, hardship continues to have its ripple effect, while the wealthy become increasingly unneighbourly, ridding themselves of the African culture that obliges them to share.

In this analysis, Africa as a whole becomes the underclass in the world's economic neighbourhood. African expertise is under-utilised, while designated experts are flown in (and maintained by African economic resources at colossal expense) to monitor the SAP these same moneylenders required the African governments to set in place as a condition for the lending. These experts help to pile up debts that African peasants and minor technicians are called upon to pay, and the interest on which the undercompensated primary products go to defray. This rejection of local expertise is both dehumanising and demoralising. (And, by the way, Church structures are not above SAP-type relationships.) SAP has no human face, thus it presents itself as another phase of the scramble for Africa. It is an attempt to complete the task initiated by nineteenth-century policies of colonial exploitation and land alienation, by so-called policies of co-operation through the financing of extractive industries. SAP has built into it a notion of surplus population, meaning those who are not avid consumers. They do not count for the market that produces profits that capital so urgently demands.

Increasingly, the money world makes inroads into Africa's agricultural economy, not only by the traditional utilisation of land for export crops, but now by the control of what Africa can plant to eat, through plant genetic manipulation that spreads hybrids around the world. How will peasant farmers manage if they cannot safeguard next year's crop by this year's harvest? Africa's loss may be immediate, but the fact that we are eliminating certain plant and animal species, is bound to affect the global ecology in the long run. The earth remains a neighbourhood and, in the end, the environmental hazards associated with the extractive industries, disposal of industrial waste and the increasing use of chemicals in food farming, will have a negative effect on our common home and its environment. The new international economic order proposed by the Third World in Algiers (1975), the Brandt commission (1980) and the 1995 summit on world poverty, all cry for a recognition that economics is about human relations and not how individuals and wealthy neighbours can hold on to the competition in consumerism while the poor strategise continuously for survival.

Faith communities

No survey of human neighbourhoods can ignore the factor of religion. Faith is a mark of human existence that affects relationships in a very real way and at a very deep level. For Christians, biblical exegesis presents one with the existence of many faiths and one source of all being, God. A good deal of the Scriptures of the Christian religion teach exclusivism, but within the

Scriptures there are also teachings that urge us to liberate ourselves from such biblical texts. The prophets and Jesus direct us to the points at which our paradigms need to shift – the people next door that we label pagans and idol worshippers. We do so from a selective and uncritical approach to Scripture that has become an idol for us. Often we do so from doctrinal positions and phrases that we learned by heart, never stopping to ask ourselves whether we understand what we are saying. Unexamined religion can and does constitute a danger to neighbourliness.

Beyond the biblical traditions are many more faiths. One is led to ask a number of questions. Can we say we have the same God? What is the reason for our mutual prejudices? For what reasons do neighbours support or frustrate the marriage of persons who hold different religious faiths? The African neighbourhood is full of these challenges. The people next door in many African countries, and increasingly elsewhere, may be practitioners of a religion other than what one adheres to. We seem to have come to terms with the fact that the global neighbourhood is multi-religious, but we have yet to actively appropriate this experience for promoting community life.

Generally speaking, Africa enjoys a live-and-let-live attitude in this neighbourhood. Often there is sharing of a neighbour's joy during religious festivals and mutual respect for religious observances. This remains true until there is a scramble for economic resources or political power. Nigeria and Sudan remain supreme examples of this struggle, but history attests to the fact that religion can be a force that rips apart neighbourliness. We have even used religion to promote violence against the other. The mutual suspicion between Christian and Muslim, Muslim and Hindu, and the contempt poured on primal religions by Christians and Muslims alike, have not made for dynamic learning and affirming neighbourhoods. Religious chauvinism, from whatever quarters, is not a recipe for good neighbourliness. It presupposes a monopoly of truth and of God and so undercuts the roots of our common humanity in a way that prevents our acting humanely toward the other. The practice of neighbourliness is anchored in a spirituality of care and respect for the other's spiritual resources.

Sharing spirituality across religious boundaries will make us neighbours who honour each other's specificities while at the same time seeking mutual caring and sharing and learning together.

Gender

One's neighbour is often not even the people next door but the people of one's home, household, workplace and religious community. One's neighbour is the person of the opposite gender. Gender can and does destroy hospitality and hence human relationship and community health. The relationship can move from being healing circles in a wounding world, to a prison of gender definition. Communities in which one's gender as a female takes precedence over one's humanity can generate dehumanisation and marginalisation. In the past thirty or so years, many women have pointed out and protested against sexism and other social operations along the gender divide that do violence to the humanity of women, tear up community and distort hospitality. We cannot avoid having persons of other gender as our neighbours, except by deliberate institutional separation. The challenge is how to create a neighbourhood that is affirming and nurturing and for which all contribute their gifts, irrespective of gender. Very often we have overlooked gender as a hermeneutical principle in our understanding of, and our journey toward, Christlike neighbourliness, and the silence has meant the marginalisation of women in the process of history-making.

The objectification of the female body and the location of sin in sexual relations, accompanied by the institutions of female prostitution and sexual slavery, have put a mantle of invisibility around sex tourism that is shattering human relations in many places around the world. Moreover, sex tourism highlights the power that money wields in the shaping of human relations. Money runs our neighbourhoods. Persons are not neighbours, they are tools, instruments, objects for feeding the ego of the neighbour who can 'pay' for the services of others who have no bargaining powers. Human beings cease to be persons with whom to relate in mutual dialogue and empowerment. They only exist to be used. They are not our neighbours, they are simply at our service, available for our use. They are at our disposal and, by that very fact, disposable.

The unacknowledged neighbour

Absence of community and hospitality develops when we do not acknowledge the existence of the other. The people next door become invisible and inaudible to us. The many isolated and hidden persons whom we simply ignore or actively marginalise, are put beyond the bounds of our neighbourliness. When we pass by on the other side, we cannot even tell who it is we are avoiding. We simply deny their existence. All who are in need of affirmation, survival and healing, tend to exist for us as unacknowledged neighbours or as social problems – never as fellow humans.

In our neighbourhood are children, persons with visible mental and physical disabilities, persons who are homeless and landless and nameless. All these and many more are human beings we prefer not to see, because they are not of our race, class, religion, or whatever is the name of the fence we have erected to mark our in-group. They are persons we do not need and who, in our view, are dispensable – or even worse, a burden to the neighbourhood. We set up neighbourhood watches to ward off crime, but we do not set up neighbourhood watches to look out for the hungry, the homeless, the sick and the housebound. They are either invisible or we prefer not to know of their existence.

Being a neighbourhood does not preclude conflicts. A history of animosity and exploitation breeds a legacy of cyclical strife, resistance and often bloodshed. Jews and Arabs, Hutu and Tutsi, Moslems and Croats, yearn unsuccessfully for neighbourliness, and the rest of the world looks on, wringing its hands. Compassion should result in life-giving action. An agitated womb should give birth to new life. The challenge is how this endemic conflict is managed. Difference is a fact in human community, but being white or male should not become equated with having hegemony over others, for 'power over', whatever its source or destination, is an enemy of neighbourliness. How do we get at the roots of endemic conflicts? We would like to affirm that these experiences of how community works, encourage us to accept variety as an opportunity for widening our circles of relationships so that our own humanity would be enriched, but how can we extricate ourselves from biting one another?

There is another angle to this diversity, variety and inequality that presents an acute challenge to our sense of neighbourliness. We often hear this articulated as one's responsibility to one's self and to one's kind. In situations of injustice and exploitation, does one cover up the evil to shield or safeguard the interests of the immediate neighbour? If the exploitation of primary producers means higher interest that pays for me and my kind, do I work against this exploitation and subvert my primary circle's interest? Is every person a neighbour? How, and to what extent, do I prove myself a neighbour to the isolated or violated persons named above? Having acknowledged the presence of hidden persons among us, how do I stay close to the victims of these societal fences that prevent neighbourliness and block the spread of qualitative living to all? Jesus did throw a challenge to his followers: 'If you do good only to your kind, what right living have you exhibited beyond human wisdom?' (my understanding of Matt. 5:43–48).

The neighbour as the self

A study of neighbourliness, beginning with the parable of the Good Samaritan, underlines for us how God makes the invisible visible. We are led into God's own method of becoming our neighbour in Jesus of Nazareth. The challenge is, what do we do after we have become aware of who is our neighbour? What does it take to love one's neighbour as one loves one's self? God is indeed agitated by our lack of recognition of the divine presence. Your closest neighbour is yourself – the self that is in the image of God. In this parable, God is revealed as the Compassionate One, the One who suffers with us. In the idiom of the Akan and the Hebrews, God is the one whose womb becomes agitated at the sight of suffering and meanness. The call to be a neighbour is a call for the demonstration of compassion, on the model and the pattern of God. God does not simply hear cries, God responds with appropriate action for transformation that brings with it peace, justice and fullness of life. Hence the call to perfection at the end of the above passage. To be perfect in love, is to love your neighbour as yourself.

Footnotes

[1] Busia, Kofi Abrefa, *The Position of the Chief in the Modern Political System of Ashanti* (London: Oxford University Press, 1951), 9.

[2] Antubam, Kofi, *Ghana's Heritage of Culture* (Leipzig: Koehler and Amelang, 1963), 42.

[3] Antubam, *Ghana's Heritage of Culture*, 52.

[4] Antubam, *Ghana's Heritage of Culture*, 48.

CHAPTER 7

Poverty and Motherhood

The juxtaposition of poverty and motherhood is so strange as to be almost offensive. It may be granted that this response is the result of socialisation and may be dismissed as the internalisation of domesticating cultural norms. In this contribution, I do not wish to debate this issue nor go into the economic discussions that link motherhood with population control and the debates on abortion, planned parenthood and responsible parenthood, as all these affect men as well as women. I therefore do not wish to link them to motherhood. What I am offering is a testimony which I believe will find resonance in the souls of many African women.

I am Ghanaian and an Akan with both my parents and their parents on both sides belonging to mother-centred groups. My political and economic status in Akan structures depends on who my mother is. I am who I am because of who my mother is. I have no biological children but I am the first of my parents' nine children. Any Akan daughter will tell you what that means. I have not experienced motherhood but I know what mothering means. I have accompanied my mother through her motherhood. Motherhood has not made my mother poor. *My mother is rich.* She has a community of people whose joys and sorrows are hers. I am rich because I have this community and hold a special place in it. I am not a mother but I have children.

To many ears this sounds folkloric, a glorification of a culture, a sublimation of instincts and many such explanations. For me, this is life. The Akan proverbs below are not just sayings, they are the heart of the wisdom by which the Akan live today and can be a guide even for the management of the political unit called Ghana. Mothering is a religious duty. It is what a good socio-political and economic system should be about, if the human beings entrusted to the state are to be fully human, nurtured to care for, and take care of, themselves, one another and their environments. Biological motherhood embodies all of this for the Akan, as for many African peoples. One proverb observes: 'When you catch a hen her chickens are easily collected'. Children are disoriented and fall easy prey when mothering is absent or inadequate. Another proverb puts it more emphatically: 'When mother is no more, the clan is no more'. It is the presence of a mother that keeps the Akan family together in that social system. 'A child may resemble the father, but a child belongs to the mother.' With such a high premium on biological motherhood and mothering as a principle of human relations and the organisation of the human community, to associate motherhood with poverty will need a very careful analysis and detailed substantiation. Mothering, biological or otherwise, calls for a life of letting go, a readiness to share resources and to receive with appreciation what others offer for the good of the community.

There are several folktales of periods of famine depicting the sacrifices of mothers in order to save their children and many proverbs that crystallise in a few words what motherhood demands of women. 'The tortoise does not have breasts, but she feeds her children.' 'However inconvenient the path to the nest the brooding hen will get to her eggs.' So women in Africa exercise motherhood against all odds. The quality of a sense of duty and fulfilment and achievement that must go with this determination to see another person become human, cannot be associated with poverty of understanding about the value of humanity. It may be exercised in the midst of abject lack of material needs and that makes it all the more a marvel that women continue to mother. Scarcely ever does one find a deliberate choice of childlessness among African women and furthest from our understanding of life is to make that choice for economic reasons.

The penalty of motherhood

Dramatic change in the economic basis of life in Africa has led to the association of women with poverty. The system makes women poor by deliberately excluding them from what generates wealth. Mothers fall easily prey to this new approach to community life that is more individualistic and competitive. When children were seen to belong to the whole family, indeed the whole community, being poor was not necessarily the result of having children. Today it can be a cause. When a nation acts as a mother to its citizens, the education, health and well-being of children are in the national budget and mothers are treated as contributing to the 'assets' of the nation. What is a nation without people to make it great? It seems such a trite observation but children do not 'belong' only to parents; children are assets of the whole nation. Poverty is put together with motherhood when women are penalised by state, religion and culture for becoming mothers. In cultures that do not understand the African concept of family and mothering, a woman who bears her traditional responsibility of mothering, including carrying financial responsibility for children of the family (even if they are her mother's children), is penalised because of western ideas of adoption. She is considered 'single' when her home is full of human beings to be nurtured and loved. The survival of these children depends on her industry and doing this has nothing to do with biology. But it is an indispensable aspect of the mothering that human life needs, in order for human community to be humane and creative.

In some western societies, women with children who are not attached to men are penalised in all sorts of ways, while in others, women have to prove they have no men in order to get state assistance for their children. The criteria is not the welfare of women and children, but their relation to the androcentric laws by which most of humanity is ordered and governed. These androcentric legal provisions have difficulty recognising mothers as heads of households but choose to invent names like 'single mothers', suggesting they have stepped outside the norm of submitting to male authority. There are no single parents (men or women) in Africa, as such persons are recognised as integral to the African family. Women-headed homes of modern times have been created by the exigencies of migrant workers, who are prevented by the laws of the countries where they give their labour and pay taxes, from bringing in even those closest to them, spouse and children.

In Africa, the instabilities of war and the disruptions of natural disasters, economic and political mismanagement, often result in the disruption of whole communities and inexorably propel women into the situation of having to parent their children single-handedly. Stateless and homeless, they struggle to care for the people who have survived with them. The global economic order that operates a hierarchy of persons is able to turn a blind eye to certain categories of human beings deemed dispensable. There are people whose welfare is theirs alone, but whose labour, when they can sell it, is bought for wages that cannot sustain life. Their salaries are determined by how much debt their governments have to pay, what structural adjustments are being made, and how determined the governments are to pay the cut-throat interest on loans they borrow from the loan granting nations in order to feather the nests of 'experts' and 'advisors' from the same countries. The whole family suffers, but the traditional expectation that women will be more caring and more compassionate, puts the burden of the situation on women. They give until they have nothing more to share but their poverty.

The impoverishment of women

The impoverishment of women in Africa is an aspect of the impoverishment of the Third World which had remained undisclosed or ignored until women themselves made their voices heard. Whatever poverty women as mothers struggle with, cannot be understood apart from the real poverty-maker, powerlessness, the inability to influence the decisions that condition one's life.

Knowledge is power, and women are kept ignorant of how, and what, political, military and economic arrangements are arrived at. Women are kept ignorant of what the drugs they take, or are made to take, do to their own bodies and to the environment. The sources and the processes of the food they cook and put before their families are often not revealed and if they are, the economic and political milieu of the producers is not made known. Even where the agricultural and industrial processes involve women, women become peripheral to the actual decisions, they are 'farm hands' and 'robots' on assembly lines. The whys and wherefores are not made known to women. Why would women submit to radiation, Depo Provera, sex selection and other hazards of contemporary reproductive technology and genetic engineering, that invade and violate their bodies and therefore impoverish their sense of personhood by treating them as objects of research and experiments? In most countries, it is women who are exploited in this genetic technology.

In Africa, socio-cultural impoverishment is more evident as western technological culture intensifies its claim to be *the* human culture and imposes its norms of what is legal and ethical on the rest of the world. Women in Africa do not fall into the category of the under-employed, if anything they are over-employed as none can claim a 40–hour week. That they are underpaid as statistics have it for women globally, does not need to be debated, but over and above this is the phenomenon of being taken for granted, of not having one's labour enter the statistics of national production. Their labour goes undocumented and therefore, in the contemporary way of looking at government spending, women are not numbered among producers and so are not recognised as entitled to consume any social services. When one speaks of the impoverishment of women in Africa, one is referring to persons whose physical labour is used to fetch them enough sustenance for themselves and their families, but who can no longer cope, because the market value of their products has fallen, or the land that they used to deploy has been appropriated by governments or acquired by those with big money for more 'profitable' enterprises. Such 'profits' do not profit women in Africa, and states impoverished by international economic injustice no longer have the means to sustain women's welfare and are the poorer for this.

In West Africa, women continued their traditional economic activities of farming, food processing – 'fast foods', making and marketing of household requirements and long distance trade as a parallel to the western economic institutions that absorbed the labours of West African men in what is known as the 'modern sector'. Women's development in West Africa has followed this line and more and more supplementary income-generating activities have been created. Women's economic impoverishment has led to a burst of creativity in domestic survival strategies. Creativity in this area is sustained by the hope that the situation will change for the better.

On the level of traditional cultural demands, however, little has changed and it would appear there is no hope for changes that will restore what is dignifying for women and remove the cultural obstacles to women's humanity. The impoverishment of women that has resulted from the joint effects of western Christianity and Islam, Arabic and African cultures, is still being overlooked. In conflicts of cultural values, women's culture and women's welfare have always taken second place. The real roots of the impoverishment of women, socially and economically, are to be found in the materialistic western culture with its androcentric laws and perspectives, for these reinforce African ones and together suppress and often eliminate women's welfare from their provisions.

I have heard pronouncements during population debates that tend to assume that only African and other southern cultures value children and put the onus on women (married women, that is, women whose attachment to men is socially approved) to provide care for them. This, however, is not the case, as the biotechnology that makes surrogate motherhood and *in vitro* fertilisation possible, is beginning to tell another story. Men everywhere are capable of demanding babies of their wives rather than adopting and 'mothering' one that needs parents. Scientists exploit women's bodies for these experiments which require loans which the men may not even help to repay. There are cases outside Africa where mothers have been deprived of land by husbands and then thrown out with their children to fend for themselves. The Asante proverb *eba a eka oni* 'when it happens (i.e. when children get into trouble) it affects the mother', can be illustrated in many cultures.

The androcentric world needs to have a continual flow of human beings, to carry patriarchal names and other naming systems. The androcentric world needs children to be born and socialised into citizens who will even lay down their lives for their country. This androcentric world expects women to be the producers of human beings, but the experience of women is that their own development and perception of humanness and the human community has to be set aside in order to be 'good women', serving the system. Material and economic poverty are the experience of many women. Material and economic poverty are the experience of many mothers. What makes the latter thoroughly unacceptable is that the system often shields the fathers from the 'poverty' that could be associated with their paternity.

A child belongs to the mother

The mother-centred Asante who say a child belongs to the mother, also say a child is the mother's until it is born, then its welfare becomes a community responsibility. The mother-to-be, however, is protected by the community. She is aided by taboos that will ensure safe delivery and guarantee her health. Inability to transform this ancient wisdom into modern socio-economic terms is at the root of the economic impoverishment of women. The impoverishment of mothers, therefore, is an indication of the inability of human social thinking to match our technological development. Human relations and development of norms of community life lag behind economic systems.

Women have fallen victim to this human poverty of spirit which puts profits before people and interests before production. In the hierarchy of human needs, reproduction of the human species has a very low priority, hence motherhood is not priced. States and other institutions have not found a way of mothering the human community, only women and biological mothers continue to see this mothering of the human race as a sacred duty. Being poor, women make their communities rich, they guarantee the survival of their families in the face of all odds. The many television pictures of mothers in famine and refugee situations tell the story more vividly than words.

God's economy

In planning how the earth's resources could be managed to sustain all creation, God was generous from the beginning. In the beginning all was good, for all was of God. The interdependence of all creation was built into the beginning and there were no 'trespasses' and trespassers, for all appropriated only what was necessary for survival and none was, or felt, exploited. Few such communities may be found in human history.

Exploitation among human beings is matched only by human exploitation of the rest of nature. Exploitation of women by the human community is mirrored by the exploitation of the humanity of mothers in families and in society through social norms and legal provisions. What we need to turn our attention to, therefore, is the poverty of the human spirit that ignores the humanity of women as persons in God's image and mothers as co-creators with God and imitators of God's management of creation.

In a mother's economy, abundant life and comfort for others precedes her own. Injustice to mothers arises from economic management which does not provide for a mother's well-being and comfort beyond her needs as a child-bearer. Even then, all is done for the sake of the child. Are mothers human in their own being, or cared for only in so far as they perform the biological function of child-bearing? The injustice done to women generally and specially to mothers, has often been described as the injustice we do to the generation to come by our wanton exploitation of the earth.

As World Bank and International Monetary Fund prescriptions bite harder into the economy of the Third World, so the face of poverty becomes clearer and clearer. When a poor country has to export more to already rich countries, it takes land from the poor, especially women, to grow what the North needs, not what mothers in the South need to feed children. When governments cut spending, schooling and health-care fall on families and all work triple-time just to be able to feed the children – so mothers eat last. When wages and salaries are frozen so that a month's earnings suffice food for only five days, husbands and children eat first. When foreigners buy their investments to put into 'productive' ventures, they grow for export, they weave and sew for export, they assemble for export and employ men, young women, older women and lastly, women with children; all of whom are paid unjust wages that bear no relation to transportation costs and rising food prices.

The anti-baby economy of the North is preached in the South, through these economic measures and quite overtly, since in at least one African country young women can only get employment in the formal sector if they can show that they are on an anti-motherhood drug. So the message is clear, if you do not want to be poor or become impoverished, do not become a mother. In God's economy, the human being is a necessary and integral part. God gave the management of the earth to the earth-beings that God created. Managing has become exploiting, except where mothers are concerned. To cope with the survival of the people whose well-being depends on her, a mother spends all her meagre wages, does extra work, or stops wage-earning if home-nursing is what is needed.

In Africa, women will continue to do all these things and more, in order to be mothers. They may not have many children to fill the earth but the delib erate no-child solution is not an option. The solution lies in better management of creation, the earth, the human community, the nation and the home, by both women and men, rich and poor, North and South. The increasing impoverishment of human communities in the South cannot be reversed by calling attention to motherhood. Mothers in Africa know poverty, but for them, the solution is a challenge to which they respond in innovative ways. The survival of the human race is a human responsibility, not just that of mothers. Motherhood gives our race the guarantee of survival. Mothers are not only to be honoured, they are to be empowered.

III. Women, Tradition and the Gospel in Africa

CHAPTER 8

The Fire of the Smoke

For the vast majority of African women there is no food without fire. I mean firewood fire, producing smoke that stings your eyes and makes you cry. One ought really to say there is no life without smoke in Africa. An Akan proverb, almost untranslatable into felicitous English but far more crisply expressive than the banal English proverb, 'Where there's smoke, there's fire', goes like this: *Biribi ankɔka mpapa a anka mpapa anye krɛdɛ.*[1]

Two 'world' wars, emanating from Europe and engulfing her colonies, caused dramatic changes in the first half of this century. This experience, far more traumatic than previous colonial pillage, resulted in a global awareness of many different historical realities and began to unmask the historiography that had registered only the stories of the powerful. Emerging from the kitchens were women who cooked in other people's kitchens so that the hostess might be complimented, while the men who worked tirelessly for other men began to drop their tools, saying they were not women. Every kind of liberation movement surfaced, as the boiling lava beneath the patriarchal calm began to erupt and a multi-vocal theme song rumbled forth like the beginnings of a tropical rainstorm.

In Africa, the eruption took the form of struggles for political independence. The smouldering embers of dying protests against colonial exploitation suddenly caught fire and began to rage like the proverbial fires of the West African harmattan, the dry, searing, seasonal wind from the Sahara. By the 1960s, young people in educational institutions had crystallised the issue as that of authority, and they demanded to know why they should not be involved in the processes that determined their lives and shaped the world. During the same period, the machinery of white racism was entrenched in Africa and the struggle against it took dramatic turns as the human species became more and more polarised into races.

Other poles began to emerge – North versus South, rich against poor – and the pecking orders that developed in-between, have become our normal atmosphere, polluted with power and the love of death, other people's, of course. Cutting across all this is the gender question, one of the oldest power struggles of humanity. This, too, has become more visible since the 1960s. Three United Nations-sponsored meetings have given the women's movement a global voice and a dramatic visibility.[2] In 1985, the world's women met in Nairobi, on the continent whose men pride themselves on having women who have no need to seek liberation as women.

While the Nairobi meeting was in session, African men were still snickering. But something new had touched the women of Africa, and they began to voice their presence. Women were standing up, abandoning the crouched positions from which their life-breath stimulated the wood fires that burned under the earthenware pots of vegetables they had grown and harvested. The pots, too, were their handiwork. Standing up straight, women of Africa stretched their hands to the global sisterhood of life-loving women. In no uncertain terms, African women announced their position on the liberation struggle and their solidarity with other women.

Before Nairobi, there had been solidarity, but it had been crouching under global issues of North-South economic, racist and militaristic struggles for power. Euro-American women were quick to name women's heightened consciousness as a liberating experience. They intensified their demands for recognition as human beings responsible for their own lives and for the ethos of the total community. But no sooner were women's movements born, than the women's liberation movement was trivialised into 'women's lib' and articulated by people who cannot distinguish 'b' from 'p' as 'women's lip'. In Africa, the move by women to seek more humane conditions for themselves was simply denied. When it was detected, it was assigned to the cracked pot of western decadence, unbecoming to young Africa. The deriding voices were mostly those of men.

Over time, African women had learned to know their oppressors, but had held their peace: 'When your hand is in someone's mouth, you do not hit that person on the head'.[3] So African women used traditional coping devices: they smiled at the insensitivity of husbands and brothers and sons and bosses; with equanimity, they went about their self-assigned jobs of ensuring life. As long as the pot boiled, men remained blissfully innocent of whose life-breath kept the firewood burning. African men preened themselves on how well-behaved and docile and content their African women were. They crowed loudly to the world: 'See! We told you, our women are different. Of course, there are a few bad eggs under the influence of decadent women of the west, but these deviants we can ignore'. However, Nairobi was different; though its full impact is yet to be felt, it seems to me that Africa must get ready for more 'deviants'. Before and during the Nairobi women's meeting, African men insisted that liberation, as applied to the African woman, was a foreign importation. Some even called it an imperialist trap that would do Africa no good.

This work is written from a Christian perspective. Two of the key words I use require explanation. First, the word 'liberation', as used here, presupposes the existence of an unjustifiable situation that has to be eliminated. All limitations to the fullness of life envisaged in the Christ-event ought to be completely uprooted. Jesus came that we might have life and have it more abundantly. Jesus's reading of Isaiah could, in our contemporary experience, be stated as

The poor will hear good news.
Those who are depressed will feel the comfort that stimulates action;
Those who are oppressed will be encouraged and enabled
to free themselves.

Abilities rather than disabilities will be what counts.
All who are blind to their own and others' oppression
will come to new insights.

And God will pardon all at the jubilee.
It will be a new beginning for all.
That is liberation.

The second word is 'church'. I am writing in the context of Africa as a person with roots in the Christian church; however, any attempt at a theologically satisfactory description of that church would take us too far afield from my immediate concern, which is how liberation relates to African women and how women relate to the church. Since it is the church I specifically want to call to task, I am broadly defining church as an organisation for performing Christ-like functions in the world. I want to examine the church's attitude to the growth of women into Christ-like persons. I speak broadly, then, of Christianity and Christian churches.

African women and liberation

In Africa, the very idea of a 'free woman' conjures up negative images. We have been brought up to believe that a woman should always have a suzerain, that she should be 'owned' by a man, be he father, uncle, or husband. A 'free woman' spells disaster. An adult woman, if unmarried, is immediately reckoned to be available for the pleasure of all males and is treated as such. The single woman who manages her affairs successfully without a man, is an affront to patriarchy and a direct challenge to the so-called masculinity of men who want to 'possess' her. Some women are struggling to be free from this compulsory attachment to the male. Women want the right to be fully human, whether or not they choose to be attached to men.

Liberation for women must also happen in the church. It was a 'church father' (Augustine of Hippo, a city in ancient Africa), who declared that a woman apart from a man is not made in the image of God, whereas a man apart from a woman, is. Furthermore, it was a 'protesting' monk, pastor, and theologian, Martin Luther, who declared that women were fit only to go to church, to work in kitchens and to bear children. So, who defines the humanity of woman? Is it the male, or is it God? If it is God, how do we get at the God-originated definition of womanness? Is family life a vocation, a demand of biology, or a convenient base for organising human society? Patriarchal systems often forbid questions of this genre.

So, in the heightened debate surrounding the role of women, some Africans are puzzled when Christian women say that it is the will of Christ (if not of the church) that women should be free to respond to the fullness God expects of all human beings. What constitutes this fullness, and who determines its dimensions? Women want to join in the search for the truth about human life and how to live it; we want to decide for ourselves, for our day and situation, what constitutes a liberating and liberative life.[4]

Given the pluralistic nature of cultures and religions in Africa and my own conviction that personal experiences are a valid source for understanding gender issues in the organisation of human society, I have deliberately chosen a personal approach to the subject. I am a Methodist. In 1835, the Wesleyan Missionary Society began work on that coastal strip around Cape Coast in Ghana where my father's roots are, in the towns of Apam and Ekwamkrom, near Winneba. By birth and upbringing in Ghana, and subsequently by choice in Nigeria, I belong to the Methodist family and, hence, to the group of churches described in these pages as western churches, a brand of Christianity that participates in the Euro-American ethos. The churches referred to as western churches in Africa are the primary target of my call to social awareness. I do not absolve completely the churches begun *de novo* on the initiative of Africans. These are the African Instituted or Independent Churches (AICs).

I am also circumscribed by my matrilineal Akan roots. My maternal grandfather, Ampofo, was, in fact, a Brong, a group that seems to have escaped all patriarchal influences. Coming into contact through marriage with the patriarchal Yoruba culture of Nigeria was a traumatic experience for me. The women from that Yoruba background have provided me with a control group, a point of reference and comparison. I cannot pretend to write about all of Africa, West Africa, or even Ghana. The living centre of my study is the Akan of Ghana, and specifically, the Asante, one of three major streams of Akan life.[5] A decade and a half of residence in Ibadan, Nigeria, and affinal relations with the Yoruba have also stimulated this study. But the sisterhood that has nourished the study spans the face of Africa. It is, therefore, my hope that this work will bear the nature of a true African child, a daughter of Anowa, the mythical woman, prophet, and priest whose life of daring, suffering and determination is reflected in the continent of Africa. It is this that leads me to name Anowa Africa's ancestress.[6]

Why respond to Feminism?

Born in Ghana of Akan parentage in a matrilineal society, I define myself politically by my mother, as do the majority of Akan people. The same is true of my brothers. Akan women are the centre of the kinship unit and girls are brought up to feel the weight of this responsibility. Without women 'a lineage is finished', the Akan say. So I grew up with a keen sense of my own importance and the necessity to play my role faultlessly.

I went through school, passing exams like any boy. I was led to choose teaching, a field I later came to realise was not very competitive, but did instil in its members a keen sense of community. All the women I knew worked: farming, trading, or processing and selling food and other daily necessities. Marriage did not change women's economic involvement. Only two of the women I knew were exclusively homemakers, although one of them had previously been my mother's teacher. Marriage, therefore, only added responsibilities to these women's lives. It seemed to me, however, that the more these women made others comfortable and dependent upon them, the more they felt alive. I absorbed all of this.

For the Akan, family meetings included both women and men. Women's concerns in the larger community were taken care of by a chain of decision-making that culminated in the *Ɔhemaa* (Queen Mother), who is in fact senior to the *Ɔhene* (King) in the ruling hierarchy. Even then, I had serious questions about how the African principles of complementarity and reciprocity operated, although I did not think in those precise terms. By and large, I could live with the system. In theory, nothing prevented me from being myself, a member of a group sharing the responsibility for its being, integrity and wholeness. Outside the group I was a nonentity; or so I felt. As a child, I had no place when members of my father's family met, but neither did my brothers.

The idea of participation shaped by my Akan background was gravely shaken when I discovered that among the patriarchal-patrilineal Yoruba of western Nigeria, a wife is a member of the work-force in 'her husband's house', but not one of the decision-makers. Added to this were my experiences of what British-style patriarchy had done to women in what we have come to call the modern sector: church, university, government, and in economic development. I began to question my mother-centred world. Did I owe westernised Africa and patriarchal Nigeria the same self-abnegation, of living for the community, that I had been brought up to accept as part of my mother's lineage? Would dying to self in these alien structures result in living harmoniously with myself? Was I willing to acquiesce to the systemic sexism that I found unjust?

I felt that I was standing at a critical fork. Behind me was a world I thought I had left behind. Ahead to the right was a global patriarchy whose tentacles threatened to engulf all human institutions. Ahead to the left was a world in the making: a world of relationships yet to be realised and maybe even yet to be created, a world full of potential for affirming the humanity of all.

I have since come to see that situation as a false dilemma. Instead, I have come to realise that by looking more critically around us, as well as deeper into our history, we can be motivated and empowered to create structures that obviate all that we have denounced in patriarchy.

The ancients tell us that as the Akan, the children of Anowa, progressed south from northern Africa toward the savannah and the Atlantic, they became thirsty and there was no water for miles around. With them was a priestess named Eku who had a dog. They came upon a lake, but they were frightened to drink the water lest it was poisonous. Eku let her dog drink of the water. Nothing happened to the dog. Then Eku herself, as leader, tried to prove to the people that the water was drinkable. She drank and nothing happened to her. Whereupon all the people shouted '*Eku asɔ*' (Eku has tasted) and they ran forward to drink. The place where the incident happened is known to this day as Eku-Aso.[7] Most migration stories of the Akan do put women at the centre, with women leading the community to freedom and prosperity.

My fear is that the way of life of the African community is turning into a reverse safari through Africa's vegetation, moving from dense primeval forest back to barren land. This is a frightening vision, for we might emerge in a dry, sterile desert, rather than the fertile green fields of Anowaland where oppression is eliminated and reciprocity is the way; we may not reach the land where variety and the celebration of all that is life-giving is the norm. If the direction of our contemporary journey is left solely in men's hands, we may not get to where our ancestress Anowa struggled to lead us; we may not reach the waters of Eku-Aso, where our religious leader Eku saved us from the fear of death by thirst.

As a Christian African woman, I seek to understand what the 'daughters of Anowa' are experiencing today and where they are going. I seek the quality of life that frees African women to respond to the fullness for which God created them. It is my experience that Christianity, as manifested in the western churches in Africa, does little to challenge sexism, whether in church or in society. I believe that the experience of women in the church in Africa contradicts the Christian claim to promote the worth (equal value) of every person. Rather, it shows how Christianity reinforces the cultural conditioning of compliance and submission and leads to the depersonalisation of women. Isidore Okpehwo recounts an African woman's retelling of the Adam and Eve story. In her version, Eve's burdens reflect her own experience: 'You will weed. The rain will beat on you there. The sun will burn you there as you think of your husband's soup. For that is what you choose.'[8] Accepting the myth of the Hebrew Bible, this African woman appropriates what it means to be a woman in her own culture and accepts it as punishment. This internalisation of the church's teaching shows its negative effects on the self-image of African women.

Like African men, African women are well aware of the impact of colonisation and the attempted Christianisation of Africa. African women are aware of bearing more than half of the life-support burden of Africa, and Christian women feel more than anyone else the church's capitulation to western norms, which it then propagates as Christian norms. This is the backdrop of the life of the 'daughters of Anowa'.

Anowa, the protagonist of Ama Ata Aidoo's drama, has never ceased to fascinate me. Anowa's dreams and her would-have-been priestly vocation haunt me. Her insistence on chosen toil as self-realisation and her ideal of life-in-community empower me. Yet, the most powerful vibrations from Anowa – and this is what most frightens me – is her final capitulation to the dictates of society. And I ask, why?

Ama Ata Aidoo's personification of Africa as a woman makes sense to me, for if there is anything that characterises the continent, it is love and respect for life, for people and for nature. And yet, nothing seems to work. Africa continues to produce structures and systems barren of all creativity, not because her sons who run the affairs of the continent are intellectually impotent, but because they use the strength of their manhood on what does not build a living community. Raped by the patriarchal manipulation of the North, Africa now stands in danger of further battering by home-grown patriarchies.

The 'livingness' of the daughters of Anowa is limited to their biology, and their sons and daughters continue to climb onto 'slave ships', leaving their mothers desolate. As this goes on, Anowa, our mythical ancestress, and her daughters, the women of Africa, are expected simply to look on, to keep the peace; they are not to seek heroic actions and/or learn self-defence, for the lions and the wild hogs and the hyenas that threaten the communal life, are their own brothers. The daughters of Anowa are expected to be supportive and to hide from outsiders their festering wounds. They are supposed to be custodians of all the ancient healing arts and keepers of the secrets that numb pains inflicted by internal aggressors. They are to pray and sing and carry. They are to tend the wounds from battles in which they are not allowed to fight. They are only permitted to look on from afar, 'for their own good'. So they stand by, shaking loosened wrists in desperation, powerlessly watching their brothers flounder.

The daughters of Anowa sit, holding their bursting heads in their hands, while their men mouth political or economic platitudes, speak the language of law and order, or pay lip-service to democratisation. When their brothers have unburdened themselves of their many words, the daughters of Anowa pick up the old hoes and their wooden trays and go to the farm to gather the familiar harvest and the firewood, so that the familiar soup may be ready. Meanwhile, the mindless talk about fruitless five-year development plans and multi-party elections continues. With quiet desperation, the daughters of Anowa try to apply ancient remedies. But from what I see around me, the ancient remedies can no longer cope with our modern wounds. They heal little, for the causes of the injuries are more complicated. This is the mythopoetic radix of my work. The daughters of Anowa, standing at the fork in the road, must determine which direction to take. As we stand there together, a myth is being created within me, an imaginative presentation of the reality as I see it, a film constantly being screened before my very eyes, my vision of the new woman in the new Africa.

Issues for the new woman in the new Africa

For more than twenty years, a number of socio-economic studies have come out of Africa, authored by scholars, both African and otherwise (but mostly others). They have begun to tell a tale different from the assertions of Africans, which are often born out of nostalgia for the past. Studies of development have been most revealing, but they have struck me as incomplete. Several writers from the North have been impressed by the position of West African women in the local economy. This traditional role is rooted in traditional political systems and, therefore, has religious ramifications. However, these connections have not yet been made.

The role of religion in the life of the African woman gives rise to many questions. Does her modern role as church-founder give her an entry into political power? What is the effect of her exclusion from certain types of religious enclaves? What is the relationship between religion and psychology for African women? Perhaps it is my bi-national (not dual citizenship) living experience, as well as the intellectual nature of my studies in religion, that point me to these missing links. With a heightened consciousness of the centrality of my ego, formed in the womb of a largely matri-centred environment, I cannot be thrown into an overly patriarchal pot without seeking a way of crawling out.

Both the Akan of southern Ghana and the Yoruba of southern Nigeria maintain strong kinship ties and constitutional monarchies.[9] Both are characterised by agricultural economies, marketing skills and the pride of peoples who know themselves to have large numbers and strong political and military organisations. Both the Akan and the Yoruba apply a primary structure of ascribed hereditary status; however, a system of meritocracy also operates, based on personal excellence, especially when a high premium on martial arts enabled people to acquire respected titles.[10] Both the Akan and the Yoruba are people who have had to contend with white culture and religion, and who, when it seemed they had succumbed, have yet managed to safeguard the things they hold most sacred: the non-material culture of religion and the ideologies on which human relations were built.

Religion in Africa, as elsewhere, has a variety of manifestations. World religions like Christianity and Islam claim many adherents and, by and large, they have become dominant religious factors in African peoples' lives. But it must never be forgotten that culture and religion are so significant within African life that neither Muslim nor Christian in Africa can be totally free of the values that emanate from the traditional African religions. There are – and this too must not be overlooked – large and critically influential sectors of African communities (among the Asante and the Yoruba, at any rate) that remain faithful adherents to the religion of their forebears. We must not forget that these persons operate entirely outside western parameters and usually ignore the attempted standardisation of national laws.

Women from the Asante and the Yoruba communities must be viewed as being under the pervasive value system of these three religions, African, Christian, and Islamic, and adherents of one or the other. Few persons in Africa, male or female, declare themselves 'free thinkers', agnostics, or atheists. We are dealing, then, with the experiences of women living in communities that take religion seriously, women who admit the influences of religion on their world-view and, consequently, on their way of life.

It is often argued that traditional African religions and cultures afford adequate and requisite participation for women. This ignores the fact of women's common experience in Africa, that by the time a woman has spent her energies struggling to be heard, she has barely the energy left to say what she wanted to say. It is true that women close to royal thrones were formidable powers and may still be. But one ought also to hear the women who warn us against basking in the glory of 'old shells', retained to govern social relationships, when the material causes that gave rise to those structures are no more, or are fast fading away.

The 'our women are not oppressed' stance is an ideological statement that emanates from Africa *ad extra*. It seeks to render feminism a non-issue for Africa. The rest of the world is expected to believe this, while the women of Africa are expected to collaborate with this essentially male propaganda. The same is true of the call to African women to be African, especially when that connotes submissiveness. There can be no agreement on who is the authentic 'African woman', not even among African women. That is just as well, and truly healthy and liberating, for all women are not one.

In Africa, our received teaching treats both 'African' and 'woman' as generic. For the former, one knows that the primary sense in which Africa may be said to be one, is geographical. Africa shares the intricate politico-economic traumas of the First World and, to a large extent, is affected adversely by these relationships. Moreover, for religio-cultural considerations, Africa may be treated as one on the basis of the similarities one observes from nation to nation. These are the only justifications for the appearance of a 'generic' Africa in these pages.

Footnotes

[1] Christaller, J.G., *Twi Mmebusem Mpensa-ahansia Mmoano* (Basel: Basel German Evangelical Missionary Society, 1879). Christaller explains that when one hears *Krɛdɛ*, you can be sure something touched *mpapa*. *Mpapa*, the dried outer cover of a palm branch, when freshly stripped, is used as rope and in basket making. When dry, however, it is very brittle. *Krɛdɛ* is an onomatopoeic word that represents the snapping sound *mpapa* makes even when it does not actually break.

2 Mexico City, 1975; Copenhagen, 1980; Nairobi, 1985. Under the auspices of the World Council of Churches (WCC), women met on specialised issues in Christianity and on human rights issues in Berlin, Accra, Venice, Klingenthal (France) and Sheffield. Other meetings included regional, national and local undertakings. The human rights issues raised from the women's desk under the directorship of Brigalia Hlope Bam, a Black South African, crystallised for the churches into the Community of Women and Men in the Church (CWMC), a study lodged in the Faith and Order sub-unit of the WCC for three years under the leadership of Constance Parvey, a white American woman from the Boston area. See May, Melanie, *Women and Church: The Challenge of Ecumenical Solidarity in an Age of Alienation* (Grand Rapids, MI: Eerdmans, 1991).

3 I was fascinated to find a version of this Akan proverb taught to Rev. Dr. Katie Cannon, an African-American ethicist, by her mother: 'When your head is in the lion's mouth, you treat the lion gently'. The African-American writer, Alice Walker, calls this coping device 'unctuousness'.

4 See Sharon Welch's discussion of liberation theology and the politics of truth in Chapter 2 of her book, *Communities of Resistance and Solidarity: A Feminist Theology of Liberation* (Maryknoll: Orbis Books, 1985).

5 The term 'Akan' is used to cover several ethnic groups in Ghana whose languages may be defined as dialects of one language. The Akan, about two-fifths of Ghana's population, divide into two large groups: the Twi and the Fantse. Of the Twi, the Asante (Ashanti) form the majority.

6 Anowa is a Fante name popular in the Mankessim and Saltpond areas of Ghana. Anoa, a variant of Anowa, is the feminine form; the male version is Anoo. I have chosen the feminine variant of Anowa for my title. In *Anowa* (London: Harlow, 1970; Longman-Drumbeat, 1980), Ama Ata Aidoo recounts that Anowa was born to be a priestess but was not formally apprenticed. In *Two Thousand Seasons* (Nairobi: East Africa Publishing House, 1973), a radical epic on Africa, Ayi Kwei Armah names Anoa as a mythical woman representing Africa. In this account, Anoa is a prophetess. Armah's epic describes Africans in the Sahara before their flight south from patriarchal ideological encroachments seeping in from the north that brought slavery and Islam. Anoa's people were characterised more by a communal instinct than a 'selfish urge for self-glorification', and more by 'peace than clamour for heroic action'. Like Anoa, they learned to hunt for food, not for war; not for pleasure, but for 'stopping the aged lion and the wild hog and to keep the hyena at bay'. Both Aidoo and Armah portray Anowa as a woman who opposed slavery and slave trade. She was the epitome of a woman participating fully in what is life-sustaining and life-protecting, someone worthy of being named an ancestress.

7 Eku-Aso, however, is a place name in Ghana. This myth was recalled for me by Graecia Adwoa Asokomfo Tewiah, a Ghanaian woman from Apam who is a veritable repository of Fante myths and folktales. Although academic linguists may label this 'folk etymology', the real significance for me is that it is told about a woman and not a man.

8 Okpehwo, Isidore, *Myth in Africa: A Study of Its Aesthetic and Cultural Relevance* (Cambridge: Cambridge University Press, 1983), 112–13.

9 These anthropological categories are based on numerical majorities; neither all Yoruba nor all Akan fall neatly into the groups to which I have assigned them.

10 Arhin, Kwame, *Status Differentiation in Ashanti in the Nineteenth Century – A Preliminary Study* (University of Ghana Institute of African Studies) Research Review 4:3, July 1968), 44. Cf. Rattray, Robert S., *Ashanti* (1925; reprint, Westport, Ct: Greenwood/African Universities Press, 1971), 35; Frazer, Robert, *The Novels of Ayi Kwei Armah* (London: Heinemann, 1980), 86.

CHAPTER 9

Women and Ritual in Africa

Africa is very hospitable. She has played host to both Christianity and Islam, expecting them to be equally tolerant. They have not been so. Because Christianity and Islam both claim to possess unique and superior revelations, they continue to compete for the conversion of adherents of the primal religions of Africa.

The approaches of Christian and Muslim missionaries, and the efforts of western colonial governments and their successors among followers of African traditional religions, have all been generally ineffective, primarily because most westerners lack an understanding of the importance of African religion as an integral part of African culture and life. Westerners have been reluctant to accept the pervasiveness and resilience of religious rituals and the hold they have on people's understanding of life. African rituals have an import that is at once psychological, spiritual, political and social. Africans operate with an integrated world-view that assigns a major place to religious factors and beliefs. It is only those who practice these religious rituals who can make a judgement about their modification or their usefulness. Africans themselves have the ultimate responsibility for evaluating their use.

By their integrated nature and their pervasiveness, African religions exhibit a remarkable similarity to the religions of the indigenous peoples of the Pacific and of Native Americans. It is important to point this out because scholars of African religion often tend to treat African religions as unique. Instead, the study of African religion through its rituals can provide an intercultural perspective to illuminate the various religions of the world.

Women in African religion

The position of women in Africa today – both within the wider society and within religion – is normally prescribed by what is deemed to be beneficial to the welfare of the whole community of women and men. Unfortunately, most of the prescribing tends to be carried out by male authorities, and the resulting role of women tends to be circumscribed by an unchanging set of norms enshrined in a culture that appears to be equally unchanging.

Much has been said to suggest that the participation of women in African religion is adequate. It has also been suggested that equality as a concept cannot be applied to African culture, since role differentiations in Africa are clear and are not meant to be valued hierarchically. Although it is true that in Africa women are in charge of shrines and cultic centres, it is also observable that there are more women in the secondary roles of mediums and cultic dancers, than there are women who serve as high priests of shrines or as healers. Even more obvious is the fact that more women than men are clients of the divinities of the cults. In the African Instituted Churches[1] women are most visible in the structures of authority. However, even here, traditional taboos still exclude women, including women founders of the churches, from sacramental roles.

Religion is an area of life that seems to be able to escape public attention. It is also an area in which individuals may be intimidated to abdicate responsibility for their own lives and to place themselves and everybody else 'in God's hands'. This should not happen. Christian feminists undertaking 'God-talk' must work for the liberation of women from an image of God created for women by men. When examining the role of women in religion in Africa – whether speaking of Christianity, Islam, or African traditional religions – we must face two fundamental questions: What responsibilities do women have in the structures of religion? How does religion serve or obstruct women's development?

The importance of ritual

African religion gives a major role to rites of passage. An individual's path through life is monitored, marked and celebrated from even before birth to death and thereafter, and the events in the life of a community echo this same cycle. Throughout a person's life several rituals may be celebrated. Starting a new farm, a new business, a journey, a building – each new venture demands a foundational ritual. Rituals include supplication rites for rain, good health, and children. There are also purification rites to expunge negative influences and contaminations that one has acquired in daily interactions with other people, animals, or objects that are taboo. There are thanksgiving rites for harvest, and for other accomplishments and festivals to celebrate significant events of a community. A brief examination of key rituals and festivals can give us insights into how religion informs and shapes women's lives, and to some extent how life shapes religion.

Birth

Birth is marked as the passage from the other dimension of time and space to this one. Among the Akan of Ghana, all the rituals of this stage apply equally to boys and girls. On the eighth day, infants of both sexes undergo operations with sexual connotations of beauty and potency. Girls may have their ears pierced and boys are circumcised. Though belonging to the Akan group, the Asante touch neither boys nor girls, as a person deformed in any way is unfit to perform religious rites. Despite changing fashions, some people from traditional ruling families take care to observe this taboo, in order not to jeopardise the chances of their progeny to assume traditional rule in the community.

On the eighth day, a ritual separation from the other dimension is effected as the baby is introduced to this world and to the human community of which she or he has become a part. A family name is added to the soul-name associated with the day and given to the child at the time of birth. Family names are derived from the generation before one's own parents and may be the masculine or feminine version of a grandparent's name, so far, so good.

When the men and women of the community have assembled for the ritual of naming, the father pronounces the name of the child for all to hear. The mother and all other women have no role in selecting the name. The actions of the name-giving ceremony, those of carrying the baby and putting water and wine into its mouth, are performed by the oldest member of the father's family and a woman may participate.[2] When paternity is disputed, the whole ceremony is usually performed by the mother's family.

Puberty

The passage from childhood to adulthood is marked by rites that in some cultures include circumcision for either males or females or for both. The central significance of puberty, however, applies to all ethnic groups. When these rites are performed, a young person becomes a member not only of his or her family, but also of the whole community, and takes on adult responsibilities and community responsibilities, including that of replenishing the race.

Among the Asante, pregnancy is an abomination if the puberty rites have not been performed, and the prospective mother and father may be banished. Marriage is not a necessary criterion for child-bearing, although in most matrilineal societies the father does have a significant spiritual role.

Throughout most African cultures, puberty rituals are performed for women by women, and for men by men. This is the beginning of the bifurcation of African society. The ritual for girls includes fertility rites, while for boys the rites elicit evidence of bravery. Among the Asante, it is significant that one of the euphemisms for a girl's first menstrual period is that 'she has killed an elephant'. Similarly, a woman who has given birth is described as 'one who has returned safely from the battle front'. For women, coming face to face with one's own blood is itself an act of bravery and part of what it means to be a human being. Although a man does not have to kill a lion to be biologically male, some societies require this or some comparable achievement before a man is admitted to the rank of 'husband'.

Marriage

With marriage a young person's majority is fully recognised, and the individual publicly accepts the responsibility of child-bearing and rearing. The marriage ritual is one of bonding – the physical bonding of two individuals as sexual partners and the covenantal bonding of two families. Performance of the ritual, however, emphasises the transfer of the woman from the spiritual power of the father to that of the husband. The Yoruba perform a ritual of crossing-over with a washing of feet at the threshold of the husband's house. This element of purification is similar to washing one's hands after returning from a burial. The bride's old self is buried with the marriage ceremony and she begins a new life 'in the husband's house'. This transition then becomes more significant for the woman than for the man, as the threshold ceremony is also a definition of territory by the husband's family. The new bride is 'hedged in' by him and his people. The Akan's main interest in marrying off a daughter is in the daughter's duty and capacity to become a channel for ancestors to return through her offspring. At the marriage ritual, the Akan will feed eggs, a symbol of fertility, to the new bride.

Birthing

A marriage is not truly stabilised until all the prayers and the rituals have been completed and a woman gives birth. The birthing chamber and, in some cases, the house where a birthing is taking place, are taboo to men. Men are strictly forbidden to share the secrets of childbirth. If the birthing is normal, no special rituals are required except for thanksgiving rites and 'soul washing' to congratulate the soul of the woman for a job well done. The new mother is showered with gifts by her husband and relatives. However, if birthing is complicated, the woman in labour is encouraged to confess her sins; she may be accused of adultery and asked to name the illicit partner. Sacrifices may be made on her behalf to ensure a safe delivery. Needless to say, unnecessary fatalities have undoubtedly resulted from what is essentially a religious belief.

Death

The final ritual of passage, death, comes to women and men alike and – apart from the absence of elaborate mourning by husbands – women's funerals are every bit as meticulously performed as men's. As departed spirits, men and women are equally powerful, and an improper funeral for either might call down a great deal of trouble for the living. Because both male and female ancestors will be reincarnated, men and women alike must be honoured in the prescribed manner, so that they might return. Women's souls, however, do not demand the demeaning of their husbands in order that they may rest in peace. In the actual performance of funerary rites, men and women play prescribed and equally important roles based on their status in the family.

Mourning

The death of a spouse marks another stage in the life of the individual, and separation rites are performed to terminate the coital rights of the deceased partner. Little has been recorded of rituals for the death of a wife, as these practices are minimal. Oral evidence indicates that a widower is encouraged to obtain a sexual partner as soon as possible, in order to disgust the spirit of the deceased wife, who will then never again visit him.

In the case of a widow, however, it is assumed that a husband's soul will not rest until the widow has completed elaborate mourning rites and has been purified. Only then can she safely remarry. For most African women, mourning is an extremely intense period. The separation ritual to free the widow from her deceased husband is marked by purification rites that may involve acts like carrying hot coals to a stream for a pre-dawn ritual bath. For some women, it involves shaving a widow's hair, while for others it will require burning of all the clothes she wore at the time of her husband's death and those she wore during the period of mourning, which may last as long as a year. The widow can remarry only after completion of a formal mourning period followed by a 'decent' length of time. Even at this stage the widow may not have a choice of husbands, as provision may have been made for her to be inherited by her deceased husband's successor. If the widow refuses, she receives no material benefit from the marriage, except through her children if the society practices patrilineal inheritance.

Losing one's husband is viewed as extremely inauspicious, and this inauspiciousness is so contagious that among the Akan, prior to purification, none of the people who stream in to mourn with the bereaved family can shake hands with the widow. Widows bound by African religious traditions have undergone many unprintable customs. Widowhood, though, usually involves three main factors:

1.   Surviving a husband attaches negative influences to the widow who may then contaminate others. This necessitates purification of the woman.

2.   The spirit of the deceased husband stays with the widow until rites are performed to separate them. This separation is needed so that she can be safely passed on to another man. The unspoken assumption is that a woman must be married.

3.   A man's soul can rest peacefully only when his spouse has meticulously observed all the rites of widowhood. Before his spirit can rest in peace, a deceased man requires not only proper burial but also a thoroughly dejected

widow who, at times, is thoroughly humiliated by her in-laws.

At death, male sexuality shows a belligerent if not a malevolent character. These demeaning rites demanded of widows have been opposed by several groups over the years. Although the rites have been modified over time, the fundamental religious belief of inauspiciousness still remains, as do the socio-economic and legal consequences of a system that gives widows no official status. In most African societies, female sexuality has no autonomous value outside of marriage and motherhood.

Rituals: a matter of religious belief

At every stage in these passages through life, a principle of religion is involved. Since religion plays such a key role in enforcing societal norms and ethics, each stage has a social significance and reflects the status of women in the society and the relationships that exist between men and women. Participation in society is thoroughly imbued with these religious beliefs, even if they are not explicitly stated. Generally, African societies have more rituals for women than for men, perhaps reflecting their view of the greater spiritual strength of women. It seems, though, that many of these rituals are aimed at curbing the use of this strength, unless its use may benefit men. For example, several injunctions issued to men who are embarking on important tasks, caution them to avoid women, thus reinforcing the belief that women shed negative influences. The failure of men to complete tasks is also attributed quite often to the unfaithfulness of a wife in their absence. Thus, men's incompetence may be blamed on ritual impurity occasioned by contact with women, women's lack of sexual fidelity, or even women's practice of witchcraft.

The 'bio-logic' of rituals

Rituals for women, whether positive or negative, are related to procreation. The survival of the human race is dependent on its female component. The conclusion drawn in most African societies, however, is not that the female component should regulate the human community, but that everything should be done to ensure that the community is closely managed by the male component. Most African religious traditions have placed procreation at the centre of the woman's universe; multitudes of taboos and rituals have evolved to direct her life and to keep her safe for procreation. Rituals of thanksgiving and congratulation are meticulously observed to ensure that a woman's soul is satisfied with her role in life. Birthing rituals of renewal and revitalisation are performed after each parturition to prepare the female for the next pregnancy. Women's lives are regulated by their biology, as if their sole reason for being is to ensure that human life is reproduced and nurtured.

Participation of women in rituals

As has been indirectly indicated above, most rituals are performed either on women or because of women. Among the Akan, for example, naming children is the prerogative of men, because only men are deemed to have the capacity to be spiritual protectors. A second principle to be followed is that food and drink for the spirit world must be prepared by persons who are free from any flow of blood, which is sacred. Blood has a dual character; it is holy but it is also inauspicious when found where it should not be. As a result, women's participation in this ritual, as in others, is often limited.

In family rituals, men usually officiate, and menopausal women do so only *in extremis* or in supportive roles. Hence, among the Igbo of Nigeria, while a small boy can officiate at the ceremony of 'splitting kola',[3] a mature woman cannot. Recently when a woman was appointed a commissioner, men asked if they would now have to present drinks to her and have her split kola. This realisation of the possibility of changing roles at least enables one to ask the question, 'Why not?'

There are many very central cults from which women are excluded, except as clients. Women are forbidden to handle the instruments of divination. An important example is the exclusion of women in the Ifa divination, which, among the Yoruba, is the most important means of learning the will of the divinities. The will of the divinities is, therefore, communicated to individuals and to the community only through men. This seems to echo the reaction of the followers of Jesus of Nazareth when the women returned from the empty tomb with the message given to them by the risen Christ. The male response was, 'These are idle tales told by women'.

Parallel cults for men and women do exist, and both practice exclusion of the other sex. These pertain generally to areas of life that are gender-specific. But whereas the women's cults do not turn public to oppress men, the exclusively male cults do. For example, when newly circumcised boys parade through the villages and town of Tiriki in Kenya, or when there are Oro[4] parades in the streets of Yoruba cities and towns, women must stay away. Huge processions of men snake through the streets of lbadan during the Agemo Festival, terrorising women. On occasion, these processions have been used specifically as camouflage to frighten women away from the market so their wares might be looted by men. Only recently have these processions been banned – at the insistence of women. It is worthwhile noting that the excesses of some exclusively male rituals are now being regulated by traditional rulers who see the incompatibility of these rituals with modern cosmopolitan communities.

Among the Akan, women feature prominently in ritual dances and singing, as in *mmommomme*, a war support ritual of singing that is specifically a female activity. When rituals are performed to show unity with the ancestors, women join in feasting and dressing up, but not in sacrificing.

There is a prohibition, however, against women wearing masks, even when the ancestor being represented is a woman. Men have arrogated to themselves the prerogative of representing the spirits that shaped the history and destiny of the community. The exclusion of women from such community rituals has obvious political and social implications and may lie behind men's unwillingness to have women in positions of responsibility that include authority over men.

Purification rituals for women are more frequent. As mentioned above, women may undergo purification after a man's failure to accomplish a task, after a husband's death, or after childbirth. These purification rituals are very often prescribed by men diviners and performed on women by women. Women do take part in cathartic 'mocking' rituals intended to release pent-up feelings against powerful personalities in the community. With little opportunity for real power, women throw themselves eagerly into these rituals, to gain a sense of power or some 'stolen' dignity.

Through its provisions for ritual, religion operates in the human community as a determiner of power, influence, domination and oppression. This complex system of rituals makes a powerful statement to women about their self-worth and self-esteem. It is often an arena of intense passion, especially of fear, and hence an arena within which those in a weak position can with very little effort be made to give up their autonomy. If women more often than men find themselves in weaker roles in religion and ritual, they will require more attention if they are to be enabled and empowered toward full participation according to their innate abilities and acquired skills.

Issues for further research

The religious emphasis on purity of sexual behaviour to the exclusion of other moral and ethical 'impurities', such as the motives that lead to excessive interest on loans or obscenely high profits on trade, is a sign of our special uneasiness about human sexuality. Until recently, this has been an area of silence. Christian thinkers who are concerned with a theology of creation should begin to break this silence and re-examine Christian fear of the 'flesh'.

Any discussion of impurity and righteousness, pollution and purification, or the link between the polluter and the polluted, raises the question of the relationship between inauspiciousness and sexuality that links women with evil and makes men the innocent victims of women's sexuality. The issue of sexuality takes us back to the 'Eve and evil' syndrome. The possibility has not been adequately examined that these stories of separation from God may simply mark a development in human consciousness toward further growth into autonomous beings who respond to God of their own free will. In the Akan tradition, the separation myth is not interpreted as sin that must be paid for by the 'daughters of Eve'. There is no call for purification through child-birth, nor for submission to the male.

The whole concept of auspiciousness and inauspiciousness is one that has been attached to sexuality by religious faiths. What constitutes inauspiciousness? Is it transmittable, and what has human sexuality to do with our 'bad luck', if anything at all? In Africa, not only the African religious traditions but several Christian churches, also operate with regulations that indicate a fear of pollution. Unfortunately, the links between sexuality and 'bad luck' are disabilities for women and obstacles put in the way of their development.

The African Instituted Churches (AICs) that have done so much to involve women in their ministries, still evoke the inauspiciousness of the energy that emanates from female sexuality and use it to curtail women's involvement. In the Aladura church, for example, four categories of people are not allowed into a house of prayer for fear that their presence might desecrate the holy place. They include a woman who has just delivered a baby, a menstruating woman, men and women who have remained unwashed after sexual inter-course, and a woman with uncovered hair. The influences of African and Hebrew religions are obvious. While a man can be excluded on only one count, all four affect women. On the other hand, the same church gives special ritual significance to pregnancy. All pregnant women members must enroll in special prayer meetings within two months of their pregnancy. This ambivalence toward human sexuality crystallises in the identification of a woman's being with childbearing. Women, unfortunately, have accepted the idea that their 'wholeness' depends exclusively on motherhood.

Women are often the keenest observers of these religious provisions against pollution, particularly in the case of menstruation. In African religion, loss of a life fluid is believed to defile a woman and all that she touches. The loss of blood is believed to render impotent or reduce the efficacy of any herbal medicine or talisman. Women understand that it is not in their interest to render either men or rituals impotent or, in the extreme, to cause the death of children, which ultimately may mean their own death. Women's knowl-edge brings with it responsibility. The association of public shame with impurity and of honour with the ability to cover up, has fed the silence around human sexuality. These are matters of life and death, and all rituals are meticulously observed for the sake of the 'wholeness' of the community.

Holiness and the wholeness of the female

Much of the misinterpretation of African sexuality by western anthropolo-gists has its source in western traditions of 'prudishness'. Prudish sexual norms have often been used by western women to protect themselves from becoming a means of male gratification. To African women, on the other hand, sexuality has a religious function. Foremost in Asante regulations are those governing sexual relations, including several that oppose rape. Asante regulations include the following: a husband shall not force his wife to report adultery while they are in bed at night; a man shall not seduce a girl below the age of puberty; a woman shall not become pregnant before the initiation ceremony has been performed; a man shall not signal sexual interest to a married woman. There are also prohibitions against lewdness: no woman shall declare love to a man; no one shall refer to female sexual organs in the presence of the Queen Mother; no man shall seduce a woman in the bush nor any other place where there is no shelter; a man shall not seduce a woman near a hearth with the smoke of fire still coming out, near an earthenware pot holding water, or near a live chicken. Some of these taboos – such as the prohibition on a woman sitting in the male section of the royal house during her menses – are anti-pollution and intended to avoid the ritual contamination of that which is holy. In nearly all of these regulations, both male and female sexuality are held to be sacred and suspect at the same time.

On the other hand, there do not appear to be any myths, folktales, or proverbs that attribute inauspiciousness to menstruation. Neither do women seem to resent the limitation on their activities during their period. The restrictions may be inconvenient, but only marginally so, compared with the impact of violations on the rest of one's life. The real issue here, however, is the exclusive focus of the personhood of a woman on her biological functions; this is generally not true of the male. Birth-giving, the first indication of 'wholeness' of the woman, is also the event that calls her holiness into question. Giving birth indicates the wholeness of the woman in the same way that a woman's pregnancy stands for the wholeness of both the woman and the man. Although birthing ensures the continuity of the race, religion seems to have developed a tendency to assign 'unholiness' to it, requiring purification of the woman after the birth has occurred. Forms of religion, including African religions and the various forms of Christianity in Africa that tend to perpetuate this way of thinking, should rethink these issues.

Sexuality, marriage and covenant

In Africa, where woman, marriage and mother constitute an unbroken continuum, the question of sexuality cannot avoid the relationship of men and women in marriage. Where polygamy is accepted, there is an unspoken assumption that the female is to be a 'monotheist', while the male acts as a 'polytheist', arrogating to himself the freedom to worship the bodies of several women. 'Proper' sexual relations for women are defined differently from the proper sexual activities of men. If we interpret sexual relations as the voluntary adoration of another's body, the distinction between 'monotheist' and 'polytheist' relations suggests a not completely fortuitous analogy between marriage and different forms of religion. Double standards toward sexual relations, resented by many women, seem to indicate that moving from 'polytheism' to 'monotheism' in marriage involves not only self-discipline but also evolution to a higher quality of relationship. If a woman's single-mindedness vis-à-vis her husband may mirror her total devotion to God in matters of religion, what is the significance of a man's tendency toward polygamy?

Polygamy is a very contentious issue in Africa, but has not, to my knowledge, been investigated from a religious point of view. Is there a correlation between 'correct' sexual behaviour as defined by the dominant society and that society's dominant thinking on 'correct' religion? A study of polygamy, which western Christians often view as a 'hangover' from 'primitive' lifestyles, may yield interesting information about its religious imperatives.

In conclusion

The concept of human sexuality cannot be examined apart from the total enterprise of struggling to understand our humanity. Sexuality is a central factor of being human and not a peripheral luxury for intellectual explication. It is so much a part of us that we fear it might compete with our sense of the presence of the Divine. In the past, this fear has prevented us from undertaking a serious celebration of sexuality. It has also engineered all sorts of ways of celebrating sexuality that burden females. A focus on sexuality in our time will help us break the silence on this subject that has had the effect in the past (and even today) of portraying human sexuality as a sinister factor and one that is antithetical to spirituality. An examination of African myths and rituals shows the integrated nature of the African concept of sexuality and spirituality. This is not a 'women's issue'. It is a community issue. It is also an issue that penetrates all religions.

As far as Africa is concerned, sexuality has been deemed a non-issue in the church, as in other Christian circles, except as the centre of morality. We need to see sexuality as belonging to our experience and understanding of our humanity and of the church. An understanding of human sexuality can contribute as well to understanding the depth of the covenantal relations that the church seeks not only to symbolise but also to live. Men and women are sexually distinct beings who do not necessarily have to be identified with the opposite sex in marriage or in other forms of complementarity. Women are persons-in-communion, not persons who 'complete' the other. There are female souls and there are male souls. We may need to reorient our thinking so that we see communion as a relationship devoid of hierarchical relations and power-seeking. When we have learned more about our humanity, perhaps we will also be able to understand what God is telling us about divinity.

Footnotes

1 Known in missiological circles as AICs (African Independent Churches), these churches have been founded and are led by Africans. Examples include the Aladura church in West Africa.

2 Africa has many different cultural traditions. It is interesting to note that among the patriarchal Yorubas, women do participate in giving names at these ceremonies.

3 The 'kola' nut is often used in rituals among the Yoruba and Igbo. It indicates hospitality, sharing and community.

4 Oro is the parading of the symbols of authority and communal discipline among the Yoruba. They are carried by night and are preceded by the sound of a bull's roar.

CHAPTER 10

Calling the Church to Account

Saying that God is male does not make the male God

Because Christianity succeeded in establishing a European image of woman-hood in Africa, owing to the fact that their first converts were slaves, outcasts and servants, a people without status in the community, the true embodi-ments of the African image had no chance to influence the new faith and the new system.[1]

There is a myth in Christian circles that the church brought liberation to the African woman. Indeed, this is a myth, a claim glibly made and difficult to illustrate with concrete or continuing examples. Yet, what actual differ-ence has Christianity made for women, other than its attempt to foist the image of a European middle-class housewife on an Africa that had no middle class that earned salaries or lived on investments? The system of wages created by westernisation has produced an elite, a class that serves and upholds western Christian attitudes, and a church that continues to mirror pre-1914 Europe. For many Christians, this description of western churches is hard to stomach, but it is a view shared by many African Chris-tians who see and experience Africa's present predicament of religious, political, economic and social chaos.

The way western churches that have been implanted in Africa look at women mirrors their Euro-American predecessors. As transplants that have never firmly taken root, they have not yet grown free of the attitudes of their 'mother churches', nor have they been able to cope with reforms that have taken or are taking place in those churches. Issues such as the ordination of clergy and ecumenism are prime examples, as is their firm attachment to nineteenth-century evangelical theology. Faced with the vastly complicated, hydra-headed challenges of living in today's world, Africa finds little suste-nance in the continuing importation of uncritical forms of Christianity with answers that were neatly packaged in another part of the world. These churches, which most often take the form of patriarchal hierarchies, accept the material services of women but do not listen to their voices, seek their leadership, or welcome their initiatives. One African spokeswoman has said: 'It is an indictment on the Euro-Christian world that African church women have no significance in the church'.[2]

My criticism of African churches is made to challenge them to work toward redeeming Christianity from its image as a force that coerces women into accepting roles that hamper the free and full expression of their humanity. As with class and race, on issues of gender discrimination, the church seems to align itself with forces that question the true humanity of 'the other' and, at times, seems to actually find ways of justifying the oppression or marginalisation of 'the other'. Although nineteenth-century missionary theology has been revised or discarded in most areas of the world, the western churches in Africa continue to disseminate neo-orthodox theology from pulpit and podium, in academic journals and religious tracts. This continued dependence on Euro-American modes and hopes is no substitute for working out our own salvation as Christians who have a particular culture and history.

Women and Scripture

In African churches, it is not unusual to hear reminders of what 'the Bible says' about women.[3] African churches, with their many variations, have not produced a body of official dogmatics hewn from the African context; however, they have developed a theology of folktalk on what God requires of women. Instead of promoting a new style of life appropriate to a people who are living with God 'who has made all things new', the church in Africa continues to use the Hebrew Scriptures and the epistles of St. Paul to reinforce the norms of traditional religion and culture. In the same way that the folktalk of Akan proverbs delineates cultural norms for women, so the theology of 'the Bible says' defines accepted norms for African Christian women.

Growing up in Mmofraturo, a Methodist girls' boarding school in Kumasi, the focal point of the Asante nation, I remember clearly our morning ritual assembly for prayers and announcements. Each girl, in turn, was required to recite a biblical text. It was our tradition to quote from the book of Proverbs, Ecclesiastes, or the Sermon on the Mount; the book of Proverbs was our favourite. Proverbs were already a part of our culture and we schoolgirls could easily get away with converting Akan proverbs into King James language and then simply inventing chapter and verse numbers. Many biblical pronouncements that have direct parallels in our traditional corpus of proverbs, such as those that deal with relations in the family, acquire a universal character, which, in turn, is cited to reinforce the traditional socialisation of African young people. (Perhaps the morning ritual in our Methodist boarding school accomplished goals other than those sought by its leaders!)

Throughout Africa, the Bible has been and continues to be absolutised: it is one of our oracles that we consult for instant solutions and responses. Although Nigeria has a budding Association of Nigerian Biblicists, 'biblicist' seems to me to be interpreted as someone who feels that 'whatever is in the

Bible is true'. This norm of biblical usage among African Christians is prob-
lematic to me as it seems highly dependent on one's interpretation of 'truth'.
I also question any uncritical reading of biblical texts, knowing something of
the fluidity of their many translations.

The Bibles Africans use today are either older versions in English, French,
Spanish, or Portuguese, or translations in local languages of these outdated
versions. Few Africans, even those in Religious Studies, read the biblical
languages of Greek or Hebrew. Among the faithful who read the Bible, the
King James translation with its heavily androcentric language, or local-language
translations based on it, have become the standard. The familiarity of these
texts is a veritable opiate that will not be easily or wilfully discarded.

To speak to African Christians on feminism, or rather, woman's being, I
find it necessary to begin where the majority of us (Africans) stand as a
people. We keep the wise sayings of the Bible and our African traditions in
our hearts with pleasure; we have them always ready on our lips, because we
believe it is for our own good and, by extension, the good of the whole
community (Prov. 22:17–18). It is most important to note that, whatever their
religious persuasion, Africans take God seriously. When an eminent Nigerian
lawyer was invited to speak about the legal rights of women, she quoted the
Bible, interpreting Ephesians 5:28–31. She instructed preachers to: 'Place
emphasis on love, honour, and care ... rather than subjugation, for love means
security for both parties – in love there is no loss of face'.[4]

The expression, 'no loss of face', raises the serious matter of cultural influences in biblical interpretation. In both Yoruba and Akan, the expression refers
not simply to physiology but to one's whole being and personality. In this
sense, it is like the Hebraic 'face', which goes beyond one's features to one's
countenance. Hence, Folake Solanke was pointing out that just and loving
human relations can survive only when the equal value of all persons is
upheld. It is the oft-announced Christian principle of *imago Dei* that ought to
be operative.

Unfortunately, biblical interpretation and Christian theology in Africa have
had the effect of secularising the marginalisation of women's experience, even
in traditional African religions. It is painful to observe African women whose
female ancestors were dynamically involved in every aspect of human life,
define themselves now in terms of irrelevance and impotence. This distorts
the essence of African womanhood. Yet, it is generally admitted that the large
dose of Christianity that has been part of the socio-cultural westernisation of
Africa, especially in terms of women's education, vocations, and the interpretation of marriage, has oriented women to accept the meaning of helper as
subordinate.

Although the Christian heritage of the biblical, prophetic denunciation of
oppression has served Africa well, oppressive strands of the same Bible do
reinforce the traditional socio-cultural oppression of women. At this point,
prophecy resumes its original character as a voice crying in the wilderness,

ignored by the powerful and the respectable. On the whole, we can say that Christianity has converted the African people to a new religion without converting their culture. It has simply appropriated parts of that culture and attempted to blot out other parts, without understanding how the total culture functions as an integrated world-view and system of human organisation. One can understand how western missionaries in their eagerness, unfamiliar with African culture and clothed in ethnocentric pride, snatched converts from an unconverted culture. Today, though, must this continue? Must the church continue to base its theology on an alien terminology, using out-dated exegetical methods that enthrone an uncritical use of biblical texts against women?

On worship

Visualising God as male and experiencing leadership as a male prerogative, have blinded the church to the absence or presence of women. It has made it difficult – and indeed, in some churches, impossible – to conceive of women priests and women leaders.[5] In the Judeo-Christian tradition, announcing the word of God or witnessing to the 'finger of God', was never a strictly male prerogative. One factor that seems to have prejudiced the tradition against women is the primal role of blood in religious sacrifice. In Africa, a collaboration between the traditions of Hebrew Scripture and aspects of traditional religion, has effected the nearly total exclusion of women from rituals; this naturally militates against women priests. Even worse, significant exceptions in Africa's religious practices that validate the contributions of women, have been overlooked because they do not confirm Judeo-Christian perspectives.

A scholar of African traditional religions has remarked that it would appear that all religions agree in principle that men and women are equal in spiritual matters, but that a woman's 'religious sense and strong spiritual craving has been utilised to make her yield implicit obedience to her menfolks, father, brother, husband'; thus, a woman surrenders herself to the man-made world in which she finds herself.[6] Rather than admitting that the exclusion of women from the priesthood is unnecessary (obviously here I am not referring to the Roman Catholic Church), there is a constant effort to evolve 'forms of ministry' to utilise the women's talents developed in mothering, motherhood and the management and organisation of homes.[7] Given the range of varying policies on women's ministry, why do not the churches seek a more visible unity?

For some women, seeking ordination to the priesthood is asking to be co-opted into the ranks of the oppressors: for until the concept and purpose of the ministry change, they argue, women's creative energies are better employed elsewhere. If the church that claims to be doing Christ's work among the people, actually repels people baptised into Christ, then we do well to ask questions about the 'Christ-likeness' of that church. If the ministry appears bankrupt in any way, it is an indictment that should not be taken lightly.

In assigning roles based on gender, the theory of complementarity plays a negative role for women in domestic organisations and in the church. In practice, complementarity allows the man to choose what he wants to be and to do and then demands that the woman fill in the blanks. It is the woman, invariably, who complements the man. Generally, the woman has little or no choice in the matter – she has to do 'the rest' if the community is to remain whole and healthy. This leads some Christian women, (and the number of Africans among them is growing), to say that women should be given the same opportunities as men: women should be allowed any vocation in the church that they believe God has called them to.

Some women have awakened to the fact that they have surrendered not only to a 'man'-made world but also to a 'man'-made God who has decreed their isolation from public life and sentenced them to serve in obscurity and silence. In debates on the ordination of women to the priesthood, it has been argued that the maleness of Jesus of Nazareth and his twelve disciples precludes women from representing Christ at the Eucharist. (I've always found it curious that the ethnic factor has not been similarly used against Gentiles.) Maleness, however, has not been used to hedge the table from women. Women can receive the ministrations of men, but they themselves cannot 'serve at the table'. Does the fact that men serve 'at table' in church (spiritual) and women serve 'at table' in the home (material) mean that the church has succeeded in making motherhood incompatible with priesthood? Why are spiritual needs separated in this way from material needs? This docetic Christianity goes against any integrated world-views, whether they are African or theological. If it is menstruation that still poses a problem, and many African women suspect that it does, then the church has a responsibility to deal with this biological function, rather than to hide from it or to use it as one more weapon of mystification.

On God and gender

As few African theologians talk about women outside of marriage or family life, there is little awareness or interest in on-going theological reconstructions of the 'feminine nature' of God. While some of us women theologians have had, and continue to have, lively debates in this area, many theologians, including Africans, have only reluctantly come to terms with the fact that to be relevant they have to discard the 'lofty' idea that theology is universal and objective; they have begun to take seriously how context shapes what one says about God.

Although the gender of God does not have a big role to play in African religious language, questions of a gendered or non-gendered understanding of

God have become a crucial point in the global theological dialogue, and the African religious experience can contribute to the discussion. However God is named in any African language, in the traditional African experience God is not transferred directly or indirectly onto human beings as the *imago Dei*. While the African myth of 'destiny' is related to God, it is not said to mirror God in any way and, if it does, the relation is with the individual woman or man and not with the abstract of gender.

If anything, the African mind contains an image of a motherly Father or a fatherly Mother as the Source Being. Individuals are directly responsible for their destinies and they are accountable before God and the ancestors and before history and posterity for how they function in the community in which they find themselves. In the Source Being, there is no question of male preceding female or appearing simultaneously in the collective memories of the peoples whose concern is with the unfolding of individual destinies.[8]

For African Christians, African religio-cultural presuppositions have meant that the fatherhood of God in the Bible does not confer any special priority on human fathers; in the tradition, the father's role is carefully balanced by a mother's counterpart. So, calling God 'Father', or using a masculine pronoun in relation to God, does not unsettle women in Africa. One could say the same is true for Christ, whose historical maleness in Jesus of Nazareth has yet to be interpreted in Africa as excluding women from associating with Christ's role or from being children of God.

However, here is where, for me, the dynamics of the interplay of words and function begin to give the lie to Christianity. When theologians and preachers begin to argue that priesthood is barred to women because Jesus was a male, I see the argument begin to fall in place and 'things' for me begin to fall apart. Why is this clan of male priests being created? Did not baptism replace circumcision? Does my baptism make me less a child of God because I do not have the physiology with which Mary's child was born? Absurd! The church in Africa cannot afford this logic, not in cultures where women are named after men (as I was after my paternal grandfather) and men are named after women. Unable to sustain the menstruation pollution argument – we do talk after all about being washed in the precious Blood of the Lamb – we are turning to abstruse arguments as to the gender of the risen and exalted Christ, our only priest and mediator before God. This is either cultural captivity, in which God's loving intentions for life ('Increase and multiply') become tied to the idolatrous worship of blood, or we have simply decided – by whatever logic we may call it – that women should not touch the ritual of the Eucharist – the blood and body of our Lord.

In such an atmosphere, the church in Africa must participate in the western debate on the exclusive masculine language of Christianity. We need to share our traditional African understandings of democracies in which Ruler-in-Council is not an individual acting alone, but one who pronounces 'what is good', after consulting on all levels and reaching a consensus showing the

road the whole community ought to travel. It may be that we might redeem
both King and Kingdom. Surely it is better to join the debate than simply to
continue mouthing what we were taught a hundred or more years ago by
European and American missionaries.

On women

Sometimes African theology, African God-talk, seems no more than a preten-
tious smoke screen that dissipates on close examination. Apart from South
Africa, where apartheid has dramatised what it means to class people according to physical traits, African theologians have not related their God-talk to
issues of justice. Hierarchical and oppressive terms like Omnipresent, Omni-
scient, Ruler, or Almighty, translate into race relations as racism and into
gender relations as sexism. Being non-white or non-male imposes a penalty,
simply for not being born into the group that is held to define true humanity.
Being 'non-anything' excludes a person from being fully human. The power
to define – to enable a group to name itself the representation of true humanity – is truly an awesome power. The person or group defined is then in a position of non-being that is only active to the extent that it is allowed to be. This
is how structures of injustice develop.

African theologians who have used the liberation paradigm to express the
church's faith have taken up these structures of injustice, analysing class
(economics) and race (skin colour); they usually ignore gender. This has
happened, to some degree, because in the rhetoric of the construct, as in
African languages, one does not need to single out women.[9] It is the English
language (and gendered European languages) that has had adverse effects on
the presence/absence of women. It would help if African Christian writers and
preachers were more faithful to their African languages, ending any ambigu-
ity in this area by translating what is intended to include both women and men
with humanity.

God cannot be said to have brought into being one variety of humanity that
is inherently not up to the mark. Our cardinal human sin has always been that
of broken relations with the source of our being, God. The result has been
brokenness in human relations and in our relation with the rest of creation. It is
this brokenness, this inability to touch the other without transmitting death
instead of life, that the church must deal with, if it is to be able to empower
women and men to celebrate each other's being and thus spread love and life.
Theology is essentially a reflection on our human experience that begins with
our belief in God, the Source Being. In Christian Scripture, as in the traditional
religio-cultural corpus, what salvages all brokenness and leads to salvation –
wholeness, well-being, *shalom*, healthy living – is what is inspired of God.

The credibility of the church is not enhanced by any exhibition of sexism in
its beliefs and practices. Either women and men are of equal value before

God, both created in the image of the One God, or else we declare Genesis 1:26 a lie. If we stand with the text, then the male alone cannot stand for God if the female cannot also do so. We cannot use Scripture to legitimise the non-inclusion of femaleness in the norm of humanness. To be authentic, Christian theology must promote the interdependence of distinctive beings and stand by the principles of inclusiveness and interdependence.

The African church needs to empower women not only to speak for themselves and manage their 'women's affairs', but to be fully present in decisions and operations that affect the whole church, including the forming of its theology. Only then will the church become a home for both women and men. Since for generations women have attempted to enable relationships and promote life, God-talk and theological education remain deficient as long as their life experiences continue to be excluded or marginalised. Male blinders have turned the African church's seminaries into male-run theological factories where the ecclesiastical organisation (whichever church it may be, Catholic, Protestant, or Independent) imprints its stamp on all who pass through. (Occasionally, there may be a female member of the faculty.) In this world of rising expectations, few people will continue to take the church seriously if it persists in preaching Christ but does not live Christ. A church that consistently ignores the implications of the gospel for the lives of women – and others of the underclass – cannot continue to be an authentic voice for salvation. Not until we can say that what hurts women also hurts the entire Body of Christ, will we in truth be able to speak of 'one Body'.

The Spirit

Whatever is keeping subordination of women alive in the church cannot be the Spirit of God. The church is intended to be the *ecclesia* of all people, women and men, across all social barriers. In the church we expect to experience 'reciprocity and mutual respect, support and protection of each person's freedom, in continuum with our freedom as the children of promise'.[10] When we find patriarchal hierarchies enthroned in the place of all this, we must begin to wonder if we are not closing our eyes and ears to the truth revealed by the Spirit of God.

We see the visible manifestation of patriarchal structures and hierarchies, whether in the church or in African cultures, wherever we encounter the subordination of women's services or a refusal to listen to women's voices. Where leadership and initiative are seen as contrary to the female spirit (or are viewed as characteristics only of rebellious women) and are not encouraged or supported, we can suspect the Spirit of God is being ignored. The pyramids of power that exist in African culture have found companions in Christianity.

The tension these attitudes generate is a barrier to unity and community, yet this does not seem to bother the church or worry the people in the pews of Africa's churches – as long as the hierarchy seems to serve the church's interests. 'Good' church women, who continue their work and service only to see their men and the hierarchy content, sacrifice their leadership abilities at the altar of the church's unconcern for women. This is a tragedy. Participation in the ministry of the church should be an exercise of responsibility and of full personhood. Inclusiveness, as a principle of community building, is severely curtailed if women are limited in their exercise of initiative and authority to women's groups, where they meet to decide, to plan, and to work to contribute to the unified budget of the church, a budget in which they may have had absolutely no input.

In my opinion, it is still debatable whether or not the influence of Christianity has been beneficial to the socio-cultural transformation of Africa – and I am most concerned with its effects on women. It seems that the sexist elements of western culture have simply fuelled the cultural sexism of traditional African society. Christian anthropology has certainly contributed to this. African men, at home with androcentrism and the patriarchal order of the biblical cultures, have felt their views confirmed by Christianity. The Christian churches have not encouraged or even accommodated women who have raised their voices in protest. Indeed, some African women, endowed with strong voices and leadership abilities, have followed their calls to ministry by founding new churches. By and large, it would appear that African women have remained dependent on male exegesis and male theology; they have accepted male interpretations of biblical events as universally and historically normal. Thus, they simply manoeuvre as best they can within these confines.

Ecumenical experience has taught me that Christian churches in the west are at least willing to examine and discuss these issues. African churches, on the other hand, declare that no problem exists. This must change. The place of women in the church is perhaps the most crucial issue in our century for the total work of evangelisation. In the words of Teresa Okure, a well-known African theologian: 'The church cannot afford to continue to preach the equality of all human beings and races in Christ and yet allow its practices to be in living contradiction of this truth'.[11] While the preaching of the church proclaims that the 'old things' have passed away, the practice of the church clings to these 'old things', instead of searching out the 'new'.

Christian feminists call the church to open up its structures, to unmask the thinking that sets up patriarchal hierarchies, and to enable the divine plan for full human relationships between women and men to develop. The linear, non-participatory way of looking at the human community of such hierarchies conceals with a tragic negative mask the beauty and connectedness with the divine which Jesus's naming of God as Father should give us. Christian feminists remember that our Christian church grew from a religion that survived because its earliest adherents were willing to die to obey their God, rather than to live in obedience of fellow human beings.

A call for change

In Africa, as in other areas of the world, the churches often wait for political crises to make statements, civil wars to work on reconciliation, natural disasters to provide humanitarian aid. The church in Africa tends to be a 'rear-action' church, rarely visible on the front lines, and often delayed in arriving on the scene afterward to pick up the pieces. In terms of being with the people in crises, the church in Africa, with the significant exception of some clergy and lay leaders, has usually stood aloof and remained mute.[12]

In spite of the pain and the ugliness of brokenness, there often seems to be a lack of concern in the churches in Africa on issues of woman's being. The church has not joined in the search for a new value system; rather, it has suggested that there is no issue, thereby demonstrating its complicity in the structures of injustice that western feminist and womanist thinkers are uncovering.[13] This position should be abandoned. The church should enable all people to enter in hope into the struggles of others, to seek creatively to suffer our way through contradictions, to cope joyfully with diversities and with the varieties of being human, and to celebrate them. Liberation must be viewed as men and women walking together on the journey home, with the church as the umbrella of faith, hope, and love. The church must shed its image as a male organisation with a female clientele whom it placates with vain promises, half truths *and* the prospect of redemption at the end of time. Wider vistas of human living are needed here and now.

Since the report on women by the World Council of Churches in 1948,[14] the ecumenical movement has been trying to establish guidelines by which Christians can build a community of women and men based on the vision of co-operation. Although many African Christians are associated with this movement, either by belonging to member churches of the World Council or other Christian movements and associations, little has happened. The literature is vast and yet it seems as if nothing has happened before. Attitudes and hierarchies die hard. When women have made progress, it has usually been by their sheer efforts and against all the odds. One thing is clear: sisterhoods (whether of market women, church women, or professional groups) have been the backbone and source of energy for women's economic and social change. The very least the church can do is to make a conscious effort to promote and support women's study meetings, as well as refresher courses for clergy and lay preachers on women's issues, in order to enable the church to understand and to take effective steps against sexism.

To begin with, we Christians who form the visible church must boldly identify as sin the suppression of the full humanity of persons by the use of generalities that in actual practice do not apply to them. In fact, generalities often hide basic inequalities. Part of our search should be for new forms of being together. Most African churches with western roots have thriving women's groups; although some also have mixed young people's groups, men's groups are rare. I have wondered why Christian men seem to have little need to talk to each other in organised groups. I know from my own experience that the 'clients' of the church – women and children – need supportive groups to survive. I can only conclude that the men of the church do not need 'to group' because *they are the church*: they sit on the official boards to direct the affairs of the body. The 'men's group' really does exist: it is the church's decision-making body, to which women and young people must be represented so their presence in the pews will not be ignored altogether.

We must remember that we are talking about more than half the member-ship of the church. Talking to and hearing one another (more than just listen-ing) will go a long way to uncovering the hurts, healing them and developing understanding of what is at stake in the feminist demand for a new and higher anthropology. We Christians who form the church will be judged by how we relate with one another as human beings, how we relate as human beings to our environment, and to the Source Being.

To make a difference, joint groups of women and men might study the Scriptures, guided by historical-critical methods that take into account both the circumstances of the original writers and readers/hearers, as well as our own cultural, political and economic situation. By doing so, we may move not only to a better appreciation of women's issues but also of what the church should be about in Africa; with its economic quandaries, political instability, poverty, oppression and pretended innocence of sexism. Then we shall begin to build a community of interpretation, breaking our old habits of treating the Bible as an oracle used by priests and preachers who tell us 'the will of God'. Small mixed groups studying the Bible and the issues of our society will work to transform hard-crusted attitudes in a far more effective way than preach-ing, pronouncements, or protests. Their very existence will demonstrate the community of women and men that is the church.

Women, it seems to me, have survived the oppressive notions of the church by looking on the brighter side. Sometimes we must laugh to keep from weep-ing. Other times, we can do no more than weep. Yet women have stayed in the church against all odds. Women continue to be the clients of the church because of their unsuppressible hope that the Christian community will bring liberation from brokenness. Women continue in the church in order to appro-priate the healing powers of the Christ who cared so much for community that he died for it. Living in community before God keeps alive their hope that the church will become a living community of women and men relating to one another and to their Source Being.

Footnotes

[1] Sofola, Zulu, unpublished lecture given to the Conference of African Theologians, University of Ibadan, 1979.

[2] Sofola, Zulu, unpublished lecture.

3 In Africa, generally, the historical-critical method of biblical scholarship has remained within the universities. Biblical models of human relationships, which fit well with the African traditional world-view, have been accepted as unchanging norms for all times and all peoples. It is not surprising, then, that anything other than a literal reading of the Bible is unacceptable.

4 Solanke, Folake, address given at the Religious Studies Conference, University of Ibadan, 1976. A selection of the papers was published in *Orita, Ibadan Journal of Religious Studies* 10:2 (1976). This journal is a particularly rich source of information of African traditional religion.

5 Owanikin, Modupe, 'The Priesthood of Church Women in the Nigerian Context', in Mercy Amba Oduyoye and Musimbi R. A. Kanyoro (eds.), *The Will to Arise: Women, Tradition and the Church in Africa* (Maryknoll, NY: Orbis Books, 1992), 206–20. See also papers of G.T. Ogundipe, 'The Ordination of Women in the Methodist Church Nigeria', and Mercy A. Oduyoye, 'And Women, Where Do They Come In?', published in 1977 by the Methodist Church Nigeria.

6 This point was made at a Religious Studies Conference (1976) at the University of Ibadan by Professor J.O. Awolalu. See *Orita, Journal of Religious Studies* 10:2 (1976).

7 See, for example, the Sheffield recommendations to the Faith and Order Commission of the World Council of Churches in Lima in 1982, in Constance Parvey (ed.), *The Community of Women and Men in the Church* (Grand Rapids: Eerdmanns/Geneva: World Council of Churches, 1983). For a discussion of how the World Council of Churches has 'managed' the discussion of the participation of women in the church, see Bührig, Marga, *Woman Invisible: A Personal Odyssey in Christian Feminism* (Valley Forge, PA: Trinity Press International, 1987) and Oduyoye, Mercy Amba, *Who Will Roll the Stone Away?* (Geneva: World Council of Churches, 1991).

8 Barthian anthropology, for example, founded on 1 Corinthians 11:3, Colossians 2:9–10, Philippians 2:6–8 and 2 Corinthians 5:21 and on the logic of the biblical creation myth, is utterly irrelevant vis-à-vis the African world-view.

9 When African theologians use the term 'man' in a generic sense, they use words like *Nipa* (in Akan), *Enia* or *Araiye* (Yoruba). All these names are generic, like humanity or humankind.

10 Parvey, *The Community of Women and Men*, 3.

11 Okure, Teresa, unpublished papers, Seminar of Women Theologians of Nigeria, Institute of Church and Society, Ibadan, 1981.

12 See Obi, Daisy, 'The Uninvolved Church', *The State of Christian Theology in Nigeria 1980–81* (Ibadan: Daystar Press, 1985). See also Éla, Jean-Marc, *The African Cry* (Maryknoll, NY: Orbis Books, 1986) and Larom, Margaret S. (ed.), *Claiming the Promise, African Churches Speak* (New York: Friendship Press, 1994). Particularly informative about the current more dynamic involvement of the church is, Karamaga, André (ed.), *Problems and Promises of Africa: The Mombasa Symposium* (All Africa Council of Churches, 1991), which addresses the challenges of structural adjustment programmes and the scare of AIDS/HIV.

13 'Womanist' is a term African-American feminist theologians use. See, for example, the essays and books by Jacqueline Grant, Marcia Riggs, Emilie Townes, Delores Williams, among others.

14 *Life and Work of Women in the Church* (Geneva: World Council of Churches, December 1948).

CHAPTER 11

Conclusion: Beads and Strands

Time was when no 'decent' Akan woman would be seen without her
beads

Beadwork is an art form I associate with my paternal grandmother, Maame (Martha Aba Awotwiwa Yamoah). She participated in the fish trade in the Asamankese market and was happy nowhere else except in church. The market was her life and she clung to it until she could no longer see to get there. In the Methodist Church in Asamankese, she is remembered for her *Ebibindwom* (songs of Africa), the lyrics she wove together from Bible stories in church during sermons and sang at home while she made or threaded beads.[1] Beadwork and singing, that is how I remember her. She sorted beads out of an earthenware pot and threaded them for legs, waist, wrists and neck. Some of these beads were traditional hand-crafted ones whose names held world-views and philosophies of life – precious black *bota* beads fashioned from solid rock, mixed in with mass-produced European glass trade beads made from sand.

I remember her drawing beads from old strings and remaking them for new uses, or simply replacing old string with stronger, new string. The latter was fast and much fun, even a child could do it when the One Who Knows How (Maame) began the process by fastening the old and new strings together. Though apparently easy, if done absentmindedly or with too much pressure, the stringer could easily lose an hour picking up scattered beads. I remember our bead-making sessions: new patterns from old, beads moved from pot onto floor, onto lap; beads chosen for stringing; beads drawn off to put back into pots; beads chipped or split in half and so no longer usable; or beads that needed just a little more polishing before stringing. Beads and beadwork are an imaginative pastime, fascinating yet functional, like composing and singing Fante lyrics. All is flexible, all is renewable.

As I look at the world of African women today and reflect on that life in these pages, I think of beadwork. When I look at the variety of beads, I think of the changing being of the African woman: my grandmother, my mother, myself, my nieces, and my grandniece: different beads from the same pot, different shapes, sizes, colours, uses, ever changing patterns strung on new strings. I hear the deliberate, gentle, instructing voices of the older women evoke the rhythm of *sam-sina*, the action of drawing a bead off the thread or pulling the thread through a bead. Women threading beads. I watch the different colours and I see a pattern emerge as they reject some beads and pick up others. Deliberate choices and delicate handling, for every bead is precious and none must be lost. Even those not needed at the moment will go back into the pot along with those we have not chosen. We appear only in beads of our choice, strung on strong strings in patterns of our creation.

I also think of weaving, of the multi-coloured, ever new patterns of *Kente* and *Aso Oke* cloth.[2] In my reflections I hear the rhythm of weaving. I see a Yoruba woman, sitting straight-backed on a stool facing the broad woman's loom. Weaving large and wide, she does not produce narrow strips to be sewn together, but a whole universe of cloth – several motifs and several colours, blending and clashing, but forming one piece. I think of wholeness, a whole being who mothers a whole universe and clothes it with love.

As I watch the world of women and see a Yoruba woman at her loom, I see a time-consuming affair, a new challenge, and I see her transparent joy. I see shredded lives being bound together by intertwining them. I see her, with her back straight and her eyes straining to join two ends of a broken thread, creating a new pattern. Differently coloured threads go in and out and some wait to be picked up from a nearby basket. The beading and weaving continue, as if in preparation for the puberty rites of our new woman-beingness. As African women, Akan and Yoruba, we work to shape our new world. Like our weaving or our beadwork, we bring it into being as we create new patterns of life based on the old.

Our world is also renewed through our songs. I feel growing tension between our cultural axioms encapsulated in myth and proverb, and the ever changing conditions that social science lays bare for us. But I am not distressed, for did not the drums say, *εsono biribi, εsono mmerεbi* (different things, different times)?

> Different things! Different times!
> Roll the drums
> Making stale what used to be fresh
> Breaking open the cracks into the future.
> The drum speaks,
> The Word rolls out.
> It is heard
> And things begin to change.

> Soon, soon! No! Now!
> All is transformed – that is creation.
> People hand craft,

Nature gives birth.
The Word transforms – that's creation.
Different times! Different things.

My impression, now confirmed by the various studies, is that there have
been areas of progress as well as areas of deterioration for African women. It
is now openly acknowledged that two-thirds of the work necessary for
human survival is done by women and in Africa that percentage could be
higher. It is important to note that rural areas remain the most materially
impoverished areas in Africa, and women, who comprise 80 percent of the
farming and agriculture workers, are the most affected sector. Young men
often move, seeking survival on the fringes of urban life. African women
researchers need to give more attention to women's development, to arrest
the feminisation of poverty that is beginning to engulf Africa. Feminism and
nationalism must work together in Africa, drawing on the resources of soci-
ologists, economists and legal experts to equalise benefits.

The traditional bi-focal structure – upheld fully in rhetoric but only partially
in practice – produces a paradigm for the re-integration of African women
into authority structures.[3] Few women have truly gained participation in the
current structures devised by men following models of western modernisa-
tion. Such women are required to serve the system without questioning and
to feel grateful and humbled that they have attained such heights. That the
majority of women do ask questions and do seek change, is the anchor that
stabilises African women's hopes. Although this is a sign that all is not well
with the African woman, it is also a sign of hope: where pain is felt, life is still
present. When the hurt of women is acknowledged, taken seriously and
responded to, then one can continue to hope in Africa's rhetoric of community.

Women in Africa have survived in large part because of their own empowering networks built on traditional culture. Some of these become specialised
but marginal groups, whose goals and priorities do not necessarily affect the
rest of the community or any policy-making body. Organisations of church
women tend to follow this pattern. Such marginalised assemblies of women
become salvific only if they engender strength and solidarity in their members
and they seek fair representation and adequate involvement in more central
bodies. Groups of African women often get society's attention only through
protest, which is stark evidence of the patriarchy that rules Africa. I believe
that only through honest and serious debate can we begin to identify goals, if
not reach a limited consensus.

It is an acceptable academic exercise to dig up, describe, analyse and cate-
gorise. One is encouraged to formulate theories to explicate the findings of
research. But to e-*value*-ate, *pre*-scribe and call for commitment, is the job of
the patriarch and pontiff, pastor and preacher, president and politician – those
who are entitled to pontificate on human affairs and to call others to a life of
sacrifice. These people's truth-claims may be born from power games or

struggles, where the position of the 'winner' becomes the position of ortho-doxy and thus the truth by which the community is governed. Yet, although I am not patriarch, pastor, president, or politician, I have gone ahead and called the church to put its house in order, and I have called my sisters to stand together to enhance our being as women. I have called for commitment because life is dear. My call to my sisters tells of my dream; it is a plea for solidarity and a cry to be free of imposed subordination.

But we all remain free to tell of our dreams if we do not allow our imagi-nation to be captive. The ability to dream, like the ability to feel pain, is a sign that we are still alive and in possession of what it takes to transform our lives – faith, hope and courage. Dreams enable the affirmation of selfhood. They allow us to opt out of power struggles and to establish communities for ourselves that enable us to experience and to enjoy our own being. They are a call to the unknown, to the desert, but with a promise that there we shall find ourselves. It is our dreams that are the heart of Judeo-Christian apoca-lyptic art, as are the words of all people who struggle against injustice and for peace and community.

As we claim the prophetic heritage of Christianity, we begin to weave new myths for ourselves from the old myths. As we break the golden chains of our belongingness, we remember Anowa saying that none of us belongs, that we are all wayfarers. At the same time, even though we belong to no place, we can belong to ourselves. We may have to break taboos on our way to new life. We know that this entails risk, and that it promises, but does not guar-antee, liberation.

Some of the strings of beads we wear feature some very ugly and uncom-fortably rough beads. We need to untie our beads and restring them so we can draw off these beads. This exercise, too, entails risk, for we may find our beads scattered. Biological gender differentiation is usually the centrepiece of the very intricate beadwork that is our lives. Biological gender is a given we cannot escape, but gender as a base for building human relations and hierar-chies, is of our own making. Thus, we can draw it out of the centre and find a less conspicuous position for it. As we have seen, in mythology as in expe-rienced life, gender as a centrepiece creates ambiguities. Male and female creator divinities simply mirror our human relations and provide no norma-tive paradigms for human relationships because they too are culture-bound.

Notions of the 'ideal woman' fit poorly around most women's wrists and are certainly not for display around the neck and covering the breasts. Such beads have to be drawn off; the wearer must remove the threads that hold them together and examine each bead to determine its value. Take, for instance, the symbolism in Akan art that says that death is female. The same culture that says it is womanly to fear death and 'a man does not fear death', also says, 'fear woman'. What do we make of all this?[4] We have to ask our own questions and seek our own answers. And we have to determine which questions are worth asking. I no longer ask who created the 'ideal' woman; I know there is no such creature.

We cannot wear beads that suggest we are made by men. Such beads – like the Gabon creation myth in which man made woman out of a piece of wood – are simply impossible to wear; for the person who whittled you into being can make you whatever size he wants or make you disappear altogether.[5] The view of woman as a derivative being is oppressive. It underlies women's exclusion from power structures and marks the diminution of our full humanity. What we are given in its place is the solicitous care of paternalism, a force that isolates and insulates us, almost to the point of eliminating our presence altogether. Maleness is presumed to be the norm of human beingness. The same human traits receive approval or disapproval, depending on the gender of the person exhibiting them. Self-affirmation is admired in a man and called masculinity, while in a woman it is denounced as selfishness or egocentrism. 'If, when it falls in one place it cools, but when it falls in another it burns, that is not good government'.[6]

The single, large bead I can string and wear all by itself is one that says, 'The full personhood of the African woman (all women) is non-negotiable and self-defined'. Just human relationships can survive only when the equal value of all persons is upheld. One area we need to focus on in West Africa is that of unequal inheritance rights, which we are quickly legalising. We women must join in structuring a fair system, so we do not become the passive victims of a changing culture. African women need to participate in creating and choosing our social forms and in selecting the criteria to answer the question, 'What is woman?' We need to challenge traditional gender-based dicta that tell us we must do this and we must refrain from doing that. These norms and taboos are not sacrosanct; they simply sustain the dominant view of life and do not benefit its victims.

Patriarchies

All criteria for differentiation of human beings stand suspect when we discover that matri-centred cultures do no more to guarantee the identity and autonomy of women than overt patriarchies. In Africa, colonisation did not create patriarchy; it only strengthened it. Before colonialism, the avuncular *potestas* of the Akan already served as a surrogate patriarchy. There is abundant evidence of the marginalisation of the African woman and the feminisation of poverty in Africa today. We must have the courage to challenge African men who refuse to acknowledge the threat that paternalism poses to the unity of humanity.

The dichotomies of dualistic thinking we Africans usually associate with western thought, begin to resemble male thinking: a scheme that enables those in power to legitimise their authority over those not in power and that sends the powerless scuttling for succour from the gods. Dichotomies enable the 'distancing' of issues and challenges, while theorising postpones action for change. We African women observe the divide-and-rule strategy of paternalism and we see a strategy we were formerly taught to denounce as exploitative and domesticating, part and parcel of colonialism. As women, we cannot join in when the African press smugly labels western feminists 'neurotic', and chastises African women, who are supposed to be spiritually and psychologically strong, for emulating them. Western approaches to feminism may differ, but the goal – an end to the marginalisation of women – is sound. However, the calm dignity of the African woman, straight-backed, head high, carrying the continent on her back, should not be mistaken for contentment. While it may not show on her face or in her demeanour, she knows that the *ebonu*, the cloth that ties her baby to her, is old and threadbare and may give way anytime.

One of the earliest remarks that started me thinking about the situation of women in Africa was the notorious, 'The hand that rocks the cradle rules the world'. I felt betrayed. I knew, I know, that women do not rule the world, that much is clear to me. Women are baby-sitters and teachers who run programmes, usually (and in Africa nearly always) devised by men that do not give women any choice in how they rock the cradle. Children are brought up to fit into niches. No woman wants to experience the agony of 'deviant' progeny. So, in the end, we usually become very effective agents in perpetuating our own marginalisation. We effect socialisation by gender. We train our children to be acceptable to their father.

To challenge this pattern, we need a new myth about becoming human that goes beyond scientific or biological origins. We need a myth that focuses on human interconnectedness as part of becoming human. Today, myths of human connectedness must mirror our new vision of the earth as a home for a single human race, interconnected and of equal value. We must recognise that social structures are created by human beings and, therefore, may be scrambled, reorganised, or discarded, if they have become dysfunctional. No culture is fixed. Even precious elements of each culture must face re-evaluation and be consciously accepted by each new generation. Principles of reciprocity, mutuality and complementarity have effectively served traditional African society; yet, in our context and time they have acquired ambiguities. Mothering, rather than parenting, has been our norm. Yet large doses of mothering ('smothering') have completed the flight to patriarchy. In Akan culture, our mothering has prevented men from seeing our real hurt.[7]

We must be careful as we work on tasks of self-definition. We must not become so busy defending positions or territories, that we are unable to move from them when factors change around us. We must not become slaves to our own creations, worshipping idols made by our hands or imaginations of woman being crafted by our foresisters. We need an understanding of truth and of the role that power plays. Our grandmothers' pots still hold precious beads, such as the symmetrical structuring of authority, which ensured that women's voices were heard at home, in public affairs and in religion. Now, more than ever, we need to expand and utilise this tradition for women's development and for the development of policies that shape the entire nation. We need to focus particularly on women's full participation in law-making, a religio-cultural area that I see as the battleground of the coming decades. We shall remain marginal if we do not seek a share of the decision-making that goes into creating and running the central structures that control our lives.

Just as Christian theologians (mostly western and mostly male) never took seriously the situation of oppressed people when formulating their ideas, so African male intellectuals, including theologians, have not given much attention to women in their various enterprises. What appears in print, however, confirms my fear that females are not only subsumed under the male, but that whenever the female is differentiated, it is often as a focus of evil. The issue of language, is crucial for women's development, self-perception, and integrity. The language of culture and religion, in particular, minimises women's presence and creates a seemingly impenetrable crust for African women to break through. The approach with the most potential at the moment seems to be community-based efforts by women and, hopefully, by the church. How else can we usher in a life of liberating love?

I do not see myself participating in a world in which human relations progressively improve in a linear fashion. Rather, I feel caught up in a whirlwind going round and round, never touching ground but continually swirling, moving on to other places, sometimes higher, sometimes lower. While I spin, the whirling storm continues to move in different directions, carrying with it some of its acquisitions from previous turns and spins.

A symbol of this whirlwind could be a whorl. In Akan art, the whorl is said to represent femaleness – indecision, frailty, continuity of growth, peace and mercy. Sometimes the whorl is portrayed as the coil of a serpent representing the interchange of life and death.[8] For me, the whorl does not represent indecision and frailty; instead, it is the power to turn and to move to different planes of life, while growing and exhibiting mercy and peace. In the whirl of women-men relations, we should avoid dogmatic truths, which become desperate attempts to turn creativity back into chaos. As the storm catches us up and spins us about, we watch carefully, we feel the movements about us, and we remember, always, what we are about. We seek to retain what is the heart of our African woman-beingness: that we be life-loving.

May we have joy
As we learn to define ourselves.
Our world, our home, our journey.
May we do so
Telling our own stories and
Singing our own songs,
Enjoying them as they are or for what they may become.

Weaving the new patterns we want to wear,
We continue to tell our tales of the genesis of our participation.
We gather the whole household and begin a new tale.
Nse se nse se o!
Nse se soa wo.

Myth, history and faith agree: people can change.

Footnotes

[1] See Oduyoye, Mercy Amba, *Hearing and Knowing* (Maryknoll, NY: Orbis Books, 1986), 45–49, for examples of *Ebibindwom* (Fante Lyrics is the official translation of *Ebibindwom*).

[2] These two types of hand-woven fabrics are highly prized by Akan and Yoruba; used for special occasions, they are made of strips four or five inches wide that are woven on narrow looms and then sewn together.

[3] See Okonio, Kamene, 'The Dual-Sex Political System in Operation', and Van Allen, Judith, 'Aba Riots', in Nancy J. Hafkin and Edna E. Bay (eds.), *Women in Africa: Studies in Social and Economic Change* (Stanford, Calif.: Stanford University Press, 1976).

[4] Antubam, Kofi, *Ghana's Heritage of Culture*, 62–92. Also of interest may be the videos, 'Fear Woman' and 'She Shall Be Called Woman', from the collection of The Africa Studies Centre, Michigan State University, and 'Be a Woman', of the All Africa Conference of Churches, Nairobi (1992).

[5] Beier, Ulli (ed.), *The Origin of Life and Death* (Ibadan: Heinemann, 1966), 18–22; Lewis, George S., *Black Heritage Unveiled* (Los Angeles: Spencer's International Enterprise, 1987), 133–34. Lewis urges African-American men to return to their Yoruba roots in order 'to break the tangle of pathology as it affects the Black family structure in America and Nigeria today'. I am grateful that not all men feel the same way and recall that it was another man, J.B. Danquah, who introduced me in 1953 to John Stuart Mills's writings on the subjection of women.

[6] Christaller, J.G., *Twi Mmebusem Mpensa-ahansia Mmoano*, 3281.

[7] One of the symbols of *Akunintam* or *Nwowabere* ('the cloth of real warriors' and royalty) is decorated with appliqués of animals and abstract symbols representing female protection of the male. It is composed of a circle with four crescent moons shielding it. See Antubam, *Ghana's Heritage of Culture,* 152. See also the various interpretations of Jeremiah 31:21–22 from its obscure Hebrew original.

[8] Antubam, Kofi, *Ghana's Heritage of Culture,*111.

CHAPTER 12

Publications of Mercy Amba Oduyoye

A. CHAPTERS IN BOOKS

'The Church in Youth Education', in J.S. Pobee (ed.), *Religion in a Pluralistic Society* (Leiden: E.J. Brill, 1976).

'The Value of African Beliefs and Practices for Christian Theology', in Kofi Appiah-Kubi and Sergio Torres (eds.), *African Theology en Route* (Maryknoll: NY: Orbis, 1977), 109–16.

'The Poverty Makers: a Critique on Patterns of Poverty in the Third World', in David Millwood (ed.), *The Poverty Makers* (Geneva: WCC, 1977).

'Women Theologians and the Church in Africa: A Study of Relevance', in Scott and Wood (eds.), *We Listened Long Before We Spoke* (Geneva: WCC; German Translation in Barbara Urhobo (ed.), *Frauen in der Dritten Welt: Text und Fragen* (Hamburg: Evangelisches Missionswerk).

'A Decade and a Half of Ecumenism in Africa – The Problems, Programmes and Hopes', in Ans J. Van der Bent (ed.), *Voices of Unity: Essays in Honour of William A. Visser 't Hooft* (Geneva: WCC, 1980).

'The Unity of the Church and the Renewal of Human Community: A Perspective from Africa', in Michael Kinnamon (ed.), *Towards Visible Unity* (Geneva: WCC, 1982).

'The Mission of the Church and Nigerian Realities', in Mary Motte and Joseph Lang (eds.), *Dialogue in Mission* (Maryknoll, NY: Orbis, 1982).

'Wholeness of Life in Africa', in Masamba ma Mpolo et al (eds.), *An African Call for Life* (Geneva: WCC, 1983).

'Who Does Theology? Reflections on the Subject of Theology', in Sergio Torres and Virginia Fabella (eds.), *Doing Theology in a Divided World* (Maryknoll, NY: Orbis, 1985).

'The Doctrine of the Trinity – Is It Relevant for Contemporary Christian Theology?' in Robert P. Scharlemann (ed.), *Naming God* (New York: Paragon House, 1985).

'Women's Experience and Liberation Theologies', in Virginia Fabella and Sergio Torres (eds.), *Irruption of the Third World, a Challenge to Theology* (Maryknoll, NY: Orbis, 1986).

'Towards A Liturgy for Revolution', in S.O. Abogunrin et al (eds.), *Religion and Ethical Reorientation* (Ibadan: Daystar, 1984), 120–38.

'The Roots of African Christian Feminism', in J.S. Pobee et al (eds.), *Variations in Christian Theology in Africa* (Nairobi: Uzima, 1979).

'Absoluteness of Christ in the Context of Muslim Claims: The Nigerian Case', *Orita: Journal of Religious Studies*, Ibadan, xvi/1(1984).

'Commonalities: An African Perspective', in K.C. Abraham et al (eds.), *Third World*

Theologies (Maryknoll, NY: Orbis, 1986); in John S. Pobee and Barbel von Wartenberg Potter (eds.), *New Eyes for Reading* (Geneva: WCC, 1986).

'Be a Woman, and Africa will Be Strong', in Letty M. Russel et al (eds.), *Inheriting Our Mothers' Gardens* (Philadelphia: Westminster, 1988), 35–53.

With Elizabeth Amoah, 'The Christ for African Women', in *With Passion and Compassion, Third World Women Doing Theology* (Maryknoll, NY: Orbis, 1988).

'Christian Feminism and African Culture: The Heart of the Matter', in Marc H. Ellis and Otto Maduro (eds.), *The Future of Liberation Theology: Essays in honour of Gustavo Gutierrez* (Maryknoll, NY: Orbis, 1989), 441–49.

'The Search for a Two-Winged Theology', in M.A. Oduyoye and Musimbi Kanyoro (eds.), *Talitha Qumi! Proceedings of The Convocation of African Women Theologians, Ghana, 1989*, (Ibadan: Daystar, 1990).

'Teaching Authoritatively Amidst Christian Pluralism in Africa', in Douglas Meeks (ed.), *Should Methodists Teach? Wesleyan Tradition and Modern Diversity* (Nashville: Kingswood Books, Abingdon, 1990).

'The Empowering Spirit of Religion', in Susan Brooks Thistlethwaite and Mary Potter Engel (eds.), *Lift Every Voice: Constructing Christian Theologies from the Underside* (San Francisco: Harper & Row, 1990), 245–58.

'Commonalities: An African perspective', in K.C. Abraham, *Third World Theologies: Commonalities and Divergencies* (Maryknoll, NY: Orbis, 1990).

'Liberative ritual and African religion', in J. Van Nieuwenhove and Berma Klein Goldewijk (eds.), *Popular Religion, Liberation and Contextual Theology* (Kampen: J.H. Kok, 1991).

'Anthropology, African', in Nicholas Lossky et al (eds.), *Dictionary of the Ecumenical Movement* (Geneva: WCC, 1991), 29–34.

'Jezus, de gezalfde', in Manuela Kalsky and Theo Witvliet (eds.), *Do gewonde genezer: Christologie vanuit het perspectief van vrouwen in verschillende culturen* (Baarn: Ten Have, 1991), 11–25.

'Women and Ritual in Africa' in Oduyoye and Kanyoro (eds.), *The Will to Arise: Women, Tradition and the Church in Africa* (Maryknoll, NY: Orbis, 1992).

'A critique of John S. Mbiti's view on love and marriage in Africa', in Jacob K.Olupona and Sulayman S. Nyang (eds.), *Religious Plurality in Africa: Essays in Honour of John S. Mbiti* (Berlin, New York: Mouton de Gruyter, 1993), 341–66.

'Liberation and the Development of Theology in Africa', in M. Reuver, F. Solms, G. Huizer (eds.), *The Ecumenical Movement Tomorrow* (Kampen: Kok/Geneva: WCC, 1993), 203–209.

'The Meaning of Solidarity', in Prasanna Kumari (ed.), *A Reader in Feminist Theology* (Madras: Gurukul, 1993), 115–31.

'Donna nera: la teologia femminista in una prospettiva africana' in Rosino Gibellini (ed.), *Percorsi di teologia africana* (Brecia: Queriniana, 1994), 263–90.

'Inclusive and Liberative for All' (foreword), in Virginia Fabella, *Beyond Bonding: a Third World Women's Theological Journey* (Manila: EATWOT, 1993), vii–xi.

'Feminist Theology in an African Perspective', in Rosino Gibellini (ed.), *Paths of African Theology* (Maryknoll, NY: Orbis, 1994).

'Women, Religion and Ritual in Africa', in John Pobee (ed.), *Culture, Women and Theology* (ISPCK, 1994).

B. ARTICLES IN JOURNALS

Yamoah, Mercy, 'Education and Development', *Student World* I (1968), 67–70.
Yamoah, Mercy, 'The Church and Education in Ghana', *Insight and Opinion* III (1968), 96–98.
'Unity and Freedom in Africa', *The Ecumenical Review* XXVI/3 (1974), 453–58.
'Women from the Perspective of the Bible', *Orita: Ibadan Journal of Religious Studies* X/2 (1976), 161–71.
'Human Rights and Social Justice: A Theological Reflection on Christian Social Teaching from 1966–76' *Religions* III/3 (Nigerian Association for the Study of Religions), (1977), 69–81.
'Liturgy for Our Days', *Nigerian Christian* II/5 (1977), 10; II/6 (1977), 11–12.
'The Asante Woman Socialization Through Proverbs', *African Notes* VIII/1 (1979), 5–11.
'Controversial Ordinations in the Early Church', *Nigerian Christian* 13/10 (1979), 13; 13/12 (1979), 10–11, 14.
'The Development of the Ecumenical Movement in Africa with Special Reference to the All Africa Conference of Churches 1958–1974', *Ife Journal of Religions* 1 (1980), 25–36; *Theological Journal* IX/3, 30–40.
'Standing on Both Feet: Education and Leadership Training of Women in the Methodist Church Nigeria 1878–1946', *The Ecumenical Review* XXXIII/1 (1981), 60–71.
'Naming the Woman: the Words of the Bible and the Words of the Akan', *Bulletin of African Theology* III/5 (1981).
'The Doctrine of the Trinity: Is It Relevant for Contemporary Christian Theology?', *Orita: Ibadan Journal of Religious Studies* XIV/1 (1982), 43–54.
'In the Image of God: A Theological Reflection from an African Perspective', *Bulletin of African Theology* IV/7 (1982), 41–54.
'The Eucharist as Witness', *International Review of Mission* LXXII/286 (1983), 222–28.
'Feminism: A Precondition for a Christian Anthropology', *African Theological Journal* II/3 (1983), 193–208.
'A New Community of Women and Men for Africa', *Media Development (Journal of the World Association for Christian Communications)* XXXI/2 (1984), 25–28. (Special issue on women and media).
'The Search for a Two-winged Theology', *Nigritsia Journal of the Comboni Fathers* (1981).
'Church-Women and the Church's Mission in Contemporary Times: A study of Sacrifice in Mission', *Bulletin of African Theology* VI/12 (1984), 259–72.
'Ökumenische Dekade: Solidarität der Kirchen mit den Frauen 1978–1988: Ein afrikanischer Beitrag', *Ökumenische Rundschau* 37 Jahrgang, Heft 3 (1988), 257–70.
'An African Woman's Christ', *Voices from the Third World* II/2 (1988).
'Alive to What God is Doing', *The Ecumenical Review* XLI/2 (1989).
'Armut und Mutterschaft', *Concilium* 25/6 (1989).
'Involving Women', *One World* (1994).
'Meditation: Jesus as source of Wholeness', *One World* (1994).
'Christianity and African Culture', *International Review of Mission* (1995). Reprint from *SEDOS Bulletin* (1995).
'Calling the Church to Account: African Women and Liberation', Excerpts from *Daughters of Anowa* (1995).
'The Church of the Future, its Mission and Theology: a View from Africa', *Theology Today* (Princeton Theological Seminary, 1996).

'La famiglia africana come simbolo dell 'ecumenismo', *Studi Ecumenici* (April–Sept. 1989), 203–31.

'United and Uniting: That they may all be one', *Minutes* (Seventeenth General Synod United Church of Christ, Tarrant Convention Center, Forth Worth, Texas, June 29–July 4, 1989), 135–38.

'La familia africana como simbolo de ecumenismo', *Dialogo Ecumenico* XXV/82–83 (1990). Publication of Centro De Estudios Orientales y Ecumenicos 'Juan XXIII' Universidad Pontificia, Salamanca (España).

'The African Family as a Symbol of Ecumenism', *One in Christ* 3 (1989), 238–54.

'Scripture goes full circle in Africa', *Response* (Official Program Journal of United Methodist Women), 22/8 (1990), 22–23, 41, 46–47.

'Feminism and Religion: The African Woman's Dilemma', *Amka (An Occasional News Letter of the Circle of Concerned African Women Theologians)*, 2 (1992).

'The Passion out of Compassion: Women of the EATWOT Third Assembly', *International Review of Mission* LXXXI/322 (1992).

'Doing Theology is being in Mission: A Focus on Women', *Ministerial Formation* 62 (1993), 2–7.

'Contextualization as a Dynamic in Theological Education', *ATS Theological Education* 1993, XXX Supplement I (1993), 107–20.

'Violence against Women: a Challenge to Christian Theology', *Journal of Inculturation Theology* I/1 (1994), 38–53.

'Il faut deux ailes pour voler', interview, *Bethléem* 5 (94), 8–10.

'Zum Fliegen braucht es zwei Flügel', interview, *Wendekreis* 5 (94), 10–12.

'Re-imagining the World: a Global Perspective', *Church and Society (Presbyterian Church USA)*, (May–June 1994), 82–93.

'The Women Partners of Jesus in a Changing World', *Circle of Prayer* 13 (1994).

'Violence Against Women; Window on Africa', *Voices from the Third World* XVIII/1 (1995), 168–76.

'Christianity and African Culture', *International Review of Mission* LXXXIV/332.333 (1995).

C. BOOKS

AUTHORED

Youths Without Jobs (Ibadan: Daystar, 1972), [a cartoon book: discussion-starter on economics and Christianity for African young people].

Flight from the Farm (Ibadan: Daystar, 1973), [a cartoon book: discussion-starter on the Church's presence in urban-rural relations for African young people].

Christian Youth Work in Africa (Ibadan: Daystar, 1979).

Hearing and Knowing: Theological Reflections on Christianity in Africa (Maryknoll, NY: Orbis, 1986).

German translation: *Wir selber haben ihn gehört: Theologische Reflexionen zum Christentum* (Exodus, Schweiz, 1988).

Who will Roll the Stone Away? The Ecumenical Decade of Churches in Solidarity with Women (Geneva: Risk Book Series, WCC, 1990).

The Wesleyan Presence in Nigeria, 1842–1962 (Ibadan: Sefer Books, 1992).

Leadership Development in the Methodist Church Nigeria, 1842–1962 (Ibadan: Sefer Books, 1992).

Daughters of Anowa: African Women and Patriarchy (Maryknoll, NY: Orbis, 1995).

EDITED

The State of Christian Theology in Nigeria 1980–81 (Ibadan: Daystar, 1986).

With V. Fabella, *With Passion and Compassion: Third World Women Doing Theology* (Maryknoll, NY: Orbis, 1988).

With M. Kanyoro, *Talitha 'Qumi: Proceedings of the Convocation of African Women Theologians, Accra, Ghana, 1989* (Ibadan: Daystar, 1990).

With M.R.A. Kanyoro, *The Will to Arise: Women, Tradition and the Church in Africa* (Maryknoll, NY: Orbis, 1992).

With Letty Russell, Mary John Mananzan, Shannon Clark, *Women Resisting Violence* (Maryknoll, NY: Orbis, 1996).

Transforming Power: Proceedings of the Pan-African Conference of The Circle of Concerned African Women Theologians 1996 (Accra: Sam-Woode, 1997).